FIRST AND SECOND CHRONICLES

FIRST AND SECOND CHRONICLES

by
JOHN SAILHAMER

MOODY PRESS
CHICAGO

© 1983 by
THE MOODY BIBLE INSTITUTE
OF CHICAGO

All Scripture quotations, unless noted otherwise, are from the *New American Standard Bible,* © 1960, 1962, 1963, 1968, 1971, 1972, 1973, 1975, and 1977 by The Lockman Foundation, and are used by permission.

The use of selected references from various versions of the Bible in this publication does not necessarily imply publisher endorsement of the versions in their entirety.

Library of Congress Cataloging in Publication Data

Sailhamer, John.
  First and second Chronicles

    1. Bible. O.T. Chronicles—Commentaries.
  I. Bible. O.T. Chronicles. II. Title.
  BS1345.3.S34 1983   222 '.607   82-23919
  ISBN 0-8024-2012-5

            2 3 4 5 6 7 Printing/LC/Year 87 86 85 84

Printed in the United States of America

CONTENTS

1

INTRODUCTION TO
FIRST AND SECOND CHRONICLES

WHAT ARE THE BOOKS OF CHRONICLES?

It may seem strange to begin a study of 1 and 2 Chronicles with such a question as that. The question, however, is an important starting point because, at first glance, the exact nature of these books is puzzling. Almost from the very start, they have had to endure an "identity crisis" because of their relationship to the other historical books of the Bible. Since they cover the same history as other biblical books, the question often arises, Why were they written? What was the purpose of retelling the same story?

This identity crisis is reflected in the various titles given to the books throughout their history.

THE NAME "CHRONICLES"

The earliest title known for the books of Chronicles is *The Things Left Behind.* It is not clear exactly why that title was given. It seems to mean simply that these books contained material not included in the other historical books. Some have suggested that the title was derogatory, that is, it viewed the books as merely a collection of bits and pieces of historical data with no real significance. Very early, however, that title was taken more positively to mean that the books contained important summaries of other biblical books. They were a condensed version of the rest of the Old Testament historical books.

Those two interpretations of that early title reflect two major opinions about 1 and 2 Chronicles. They have been ignored by many as merely an incomplete version of the biblical historical books, but have been prized by others as a much needed summary of the wealth of biblical history. There are few today who would not welcome such a condensed version of the Bible.

The books of Chronicles have another name in most copies of the Hebrew Bible: *Daily Matters,* which is a way of saying that they are like the official annals mentioned by the same name throughout the other historical books (Esther 2:23; 1 Kings 14:19). It is from that title that the English title *Chronicles* is derived. By naming the books *Chronicles,* emphasis is put on the nature of the subject matter: the recounting of important affairs in the lives of Israel's kings.

The titles of the books point in two important directions for understanding their nature. The title *Daily Matters* points out that the primary subject matter is the history of Israel's kings. The title *The Things Left Behind* points out that the books are largely concerned with retracing the same historical events covered in other biblical books.

THE PURPOSE OF THE BOOKS

The fact that 1 and 2 Chronicles covers so much of the same territory as the other biblical historical books raises the question of purpose. Why retell the same events? There are two basic answers to that question. The first is that the writer wanted to give his readers another version of those events. Anyone who has both witnessed an event and read a news report of it knows how much the meaning and sense of that event lies in the reporting. By providing a second picture of

Israel's history, therefore, a fuller appreciation and understanding of those events is given by the chronicler. In that respect, his purpose can be compared with the four gospels in the New Testament. Each gospel gives a picture of Jesus Christ. Each has its point of view and presents the life and teachings of Jesus from that perspective. The result of the four gospels is a deeper and richer picture of Jesus.

There is, however, another answer to the question. It is possible that the writer's purpose was not simply to retell these events but to explain and expound on their meaning in Israel's history. Just as there are commentaries today for the books of the Bible, so also within the Bible itself are commentaries. First and Second Chronicles may then be a commentary on the historical books.

In the final analysis, the author's purpose is perhaps best stated as a combination of those two approaches; that is, to give his readers another view of the history of Israel, and to provide further explanation of the events already recorded in Genesis through 1 and 2 Kings.

THE LITERARY STYLE OF THE BOOKS

There are many kinds of literature in the Bible. However, nearly all the books of the Bible can be grouped into two basic styles: historical narrative and poetry. Although 1 and 2 Chronicles contain some poetic texts, their primary style is historical narrative.

Historical narrative has several distinct features that contribute to its use by the biblical authors. Its most basic feature is its concern to recount God's great working in past events. Though its concern is to recount past deeds and events, the writers of historical narrative are never interested merely in what happened. Their interest in the past stems from the significance those past events have for the present and future. Historical narrative then contains not only a record of past events, but also a lesson for the present.

How does the author of a historical narrative develop and deliver his message? He does it by making his history tell a story, which is able to teach his lesson.

The biblical writers were skilled in the art of weaving the facts and figures of history into a story that pulsated with life. They were gifted writers and their historical stories still surpass the greatest of the world's literature.

In attempting to understand the biblical historians' craft, two essential components of their historical narratives must be kept clearly in view. The first is the principle of selectivity. It is not possible or desirable to record every event from the past. As the apostle John said, "And there are also many other things which Jesus did, which if they were written in detail, I suppose that even the world itself would not contain the books which were written" (John 21:25). The historian must select what events to include and exclude. That selection determines the message his story will convey. Again the apostle John illustrated this dimension of historical narrative when he said, "Many other signs therefore Jesus also performed in the presence of the disciples, which are not written in this book; but these things have been written that you may believe that Jesus is the Christ, the Son of God; and that believing you may have life in His name" (John 20:30-31).

There is a second component to the message of a historical narrative. It is the work of arranging the events of history into the shape of a story. A historical story, like any story, must carry its reader along the most meaningful path to its conclusion. The reader must be given an introduction to the main characters of the story. Since stories consist of plot elements such as conflict, tension, anticipation, and resolution, the biblical historian had to be sensitive to those elements in the events themselves to ensure that in the formation of his story all the meaningful elements would be given their proper place.

The skill of the biblical writers in building their stories of history is attested in the appeal those histories have had through the ages. A story can travel through nearly any cultural barrier and can be appreciated by young and old alike.

THE MESSAGE OF THE BOOKS

The message of 1 and 2 Chronicles is derived from the development of several important biblical themes.

THE DAVIDIC KINGSHIP

The writer is very explicit about the importance of the Davidic kingship. It is through the house of David that God has chosen to bring about His promise of blessing for all men. The formula for blessing is also clear: when the king trusts and obeys God, God gives His people rest. Just as in the other historical books of the Bible, it is taken for granted that when the king is faithful and obedient, the people will also trust and obey. The chronicler goes to great pains to show the importance of godly leadership. Without a leader the people will perish. David and his house are the channel through which God's appointed leader is to come.

The message of Chronicles is "messianic"; that is, it looks forward to the coming King who will rule over God's people forever. In the historical books, the Psalms, and the prophets, the term *Messiah* stands for the Davidic King. The centrality of the Davidic king in the narrative therefore makes this story "messianic." It is the Messiah, the Christ, the Son of David, who will bring peace to His own people and blessing to all men. In the New Testament we learn that this King's name is Jesus.

THE COVENANT

The covenant was a bond that united God and His people. It was an agreement of loyalty and a commitment of love. Out of that bond arose certain responsibilities. Israel was to trust God and to obey His will. God, on His part, promised to remain faithful and give the people rest. As a father, the Lord punished His sons when they rebelled, stood close by them when danger threatened, and sought their obedient submission to His own all-knowing will.

For the chronicler, nothing was as important as trust and obedience; nothing was so hazardous as doubt and rebellion.

THE TEMPLE

The covenant between God and Israel meant that the Lord Himself had chosen to dwell among His people. Provision for the presence of the Holy God among His people had been the concern of much of the early writings of Scripture. God was to dwell among His people by being present with them in the Temple. His presence was a gift of grace and Israel was always to treat God as holy.

Because the Temple was the focal point of God's presence, the establishment and preservation of the Temple and the order of worship were important elements. Both David and Solomon were instrumental in the establishment of the Temple, and its preservation was the concern of every good king to follow. If there was one outstanding trait of a good Davidic king, it was his zeal for the Temple of the Lord. Through the Temple, God was present with His people.

THE NATIONS

Behind the themes of Davidic kingship, the covenant, and the Temple, a larger theme is being set into motion. That larger theme is the notion that God's dealings and promises of blessing do not end with the one nation Israel, but extend to all the nations of the earth. God's purpose is to bless all nations through the establishment of His kingdom in Jerusalem.

The Davidic king is to reign in Jerusalem, the presence of God is to be manifest in the Temple, and there the covenant people are to worship Him. For the chronicler, however, this scene is incomplete without the nations of the earth also participating in the praise. He, like his near contemporary Zechariah, awaits the time when "many peoples and mighty nations will come to seek the LORD of hosts in Jerusalem and to entreat the favor of the Lord" (Zech. 8:22).

THE DATE AND AUTHORSHIP OF THE BOOKS

Neither the date of writing nor the identity of the author is given in either 1 or 2 Chronicles. An early Jewish tradition names Ezra as the author of the books, but there is no evidence to support or refute that tradition. Some have argued that 1 and 2 Chronicles were at one time a part of the books of Ezra and Nehemiah, but that, too, cannot be sufficiently supported. Certainly in the present editions of the Hebrew Bible, 1 and 2 Chronicles are treated as one book, distinct from Ezra and Nehemiah.

There is also no agreement today about the date of the book. It seems safe to say, on the basis of the genealogies in the book, that the book was written during the second or third generation after the exile. That would put the date of the book somewhere in the fifth century B.C.

During that period of Israel's history, the ancient world was in the hands of the powerful Persian Empire. All that remained of the great Israelite kingdom under David and Solomon was the small province of Judah. The Davidic kingship had been replaced by a provincial governor appointed by the Persian king. The Temple, once destroyed, had been rebuilt, but not with the splendor of the former Temple of Solomon. By anyone's standards, the fifth century was hardly a golden age for the people of God. Their future as a kingdom and a distinct people of God, in fact, seemed bleaker at that moment than perhaps ever before. To make matters worse, it followed on the heels of the excitement of the return from exile and the anticipation of the coming messianic kingdom that accompanied the return.

To their own generation, the books of Chronicles were a vivid reminder of the hope that rested in the faithfulness of God. They were reminders that the Lord had made a promise to the world and to the house of David. The promise was of peace and prosperity, and the channel of the fulfillment of the promise was the covenant people of God, Israel. The books, in that setting, were a call for trust and obedience on the part of God's people: "If my people, which are called by my name, shall humble themselves, and pray, and seek my face, and turn from their wicked ways; then will I hear from heaven, and will forgive their sin, and will heal their land" (2 Chron. 7:14, KJV).*

SUMMARY OF THE CONTENTS OF THE BOOKS

Chronicles begins with the first man, Adam, and ends with the first great ruler of mankind, the Persian king Cyrus. At the heart of these books, however, are two other great men: the Israelite king David, and his son Solomon. Thus, the content of the books is framed within the names of four great men. Two of those men, David and Solomon, play leading roles in the drama of redemption and blessing that binds together the events of Israel's history. The other two men, Adam and Cyrus, formed, in the author's day, the beginning and culmination of all the families of the earth for whom God's redemption and blessing was intended.

1 CHRONICLES 1-9

First Chronicles opens with a long list of names and descendants (genealogy). The list begins with Adam and is carried through to the writer's own day. In biblical books, as the gospels of Matthew and Luke show, those lists of names and descendants were considered an important starting point for

---

*King James Version.

serious histories. The lists are of various kinds, and care must be given to the significance of each list of names. If they were not important, they would not have been included in this historical narrative.

1 CHRONICLES 10-29

The remainder of 1 Chronicles is concerned with the events and accomplishments in the life of David the king. Following the account of the death of Saul in chapter 10, the writer centers his attention on two important areas of David's career: his military victories, and his preparation for the building of the Temple in Jerusalem. David fought wars with Israel's enemies so that his people could dwell safely in the land. When he had won the peace, David turned his attention to the provision for the worship of God. He moved the Ark of the Covenant to Jerusalem and made the necessary preparations for building a permanent Temple. It was God's plan, however, that Solomon, not David, build the Temple. So David ended his days content in making the final preparations for his son Solomon's construction of the Temple.

2 CHRONICLES 1-9

Second Chronicles opens with the narrative of the reign of Solomon. The central concern of Solomon's activities in these chapters is his building and dedication of the Temple. Not only was Solomon the one who built the Temple, he was also the one known throughout the ancient world for his wisdom. The chronicler concludes his account of Solomon's reign with the visit of the Queen of Sheba, showing that the report of Solomon's wisdom had reached the ends of the earth.

2 CHRONICLES 10-36

The writer devotes the last chapters of his book to the history of the Davidic dynasty. After Solomon, the kingdom built by David all but fell to ruin. Solomon's son Rehoboam began his reign with a crisis that left the house of David in control of only the tribe of Judah and a few remaining tribes. The bulk of the kingdom lay in the hands of Solomon's rival, Jeroboam. Because that Northern Kingdom lay outside the province of the Davidic dynasty, the author bypasses most of its history in favor of a more detailed treatment of the Southern Kingdom, Judah. The history of the Southern Kingdom is recounted to its end: the Babylonian captivity. Second Chronicles ends with the edict of the Persian king Cyrus, which he announced after the exile and the rebuilding of the Temple in Jerusalem.

2

ANCESTRY OF ISRAEL

I. NAMES AND GENEALOGIES (1 Chronicles 1:1—10:14)

For most readers of 1 Chronicles, the temptation to skip over these chapters is too great. Although it is true that the weightier sections are yet to follow, the purpose for including these names was to show that God's plan was carried out by God's people in God's way.

A. THE LINEAGE OF DAVID (1:1—3:24)

The writer begins his work with an introduction to the house of David. The use of genealogical lists to set the stage of historical narrative is well known in both the Old Testament (Genesis) and the New Testament (Matthew and Luke). Just as Luke's gospel traces the lineage of Jesus (the son of David) back to Adam (Luke 3:38), so also the writer traces David's lineage to Adam. What purpose does he have in drawing the line between Adam and the house of David?

One of the overarching themes of 1 and 2 Chronicles is that the Davidic kingship is to be the instrument of God's promised salvation and blessing. The writer seems especially concerned to show that this salvation and blessing is not just for God's people, Israel, but also for all mankind. It is "to the Jew first and also to the Greek" (Rom. 1:16). That is shown throughout these books in a number of ways. Here, at the outset, it is made clear that the house of David is of the house of Abraham, a descendant of Adam. By working through the descendants of David, God is reaching to all mankind. By recognizing the house of David as also of the lineage of Adam, the chronicler is very close in his thinking to the apostle Paul, who saw in Jesus Christ "the last Adam" (1 Cor. 15:45).

The chronicler may have still further reasons for drawing the line between Adam and the house of David. As is often the case, he may be giving an inspired comment on the Genesis account of the first man. In that account, Adam sinned and fell under the curse (Gen. 3:1-19). In the midst of the pronouncement of death, however, God gave a promise of life: "And I will put enmity between you [the serpent] and the woman, and between your seed and her seed; He shall bruise you on the head, and you shall bruise him on the heel" (Gen. 3:15). The promised salvation and blessing was to come through the seed of the woman: humanity. The purpose of this first genealogical introduction, then, may have been to draw out the consequences of the promise in Genesis 3:15. It is true that the book of Genesis is careful to follow this same line, and that ultimately the historical books of the Old Testament work in unison to connect the house of David with the promise to Eve in Genesis 3. The chronicler's enthusiasm for making that point clear, however, is seen in his breathtaking brevity in tracing the line from Adam to David and beyond.

The fact that he moves beyond David in this beginning genealogy, and in 3:19-24 extends the list of the house of David even into the post-exilic period, suggests that there is still more that can be said about the purpose of this genealogy. After the Exile, the kingdom of David is gone. Kingship lies not in the hand of a descendant of David, but in the hand of Cyrus, the ruler of the Persian Empire. However, the hope that God will fulfill His promise of blessing does not rest on the present political circumstances, but on the faithfulness of God. The fact that the Davidic house still exists in the writer's own day is a testimony to God's faithfulness. The house of David may be a "fallen booth," but God is faithful and will one day "raise up its ruins, and rebuild it as in the days of old" (Amos 9:11).

The chronicler's hope in the house of David can be compared with the similar hope of his contemporary Haggai in addressing the Davidic descendant Zerubbabel in the early days of the return from Babylon: "Speak to Zerubbabel governor Judah saying, 'I am going to shake the heavens and the earth. And I will overthrow the thrones of kingdoms and destroy the power of the kingdoms of the nations; and I will overthrow the chariots and their riders, and the horses and their riders will go down, every one by the sword of another' " (Hag. 2:21-22).

It is that kind of faith in the promises of God that moves the chronicler to begin his work with a line from Adam to David and from David to the traces of the "fallen booth of David" (Amos 9:11) in his own day. He knows that God works through weakness, not strength, and that "the Lord's loyal love is never consumed, His mercies are never exhausted. They are new every morning. Great is thy faithfulness [to the house of David]" (Lam. 3:22-23, author's translation).

B. THE HOUSE OF ISRAEL (4:1—7:40)

Having placed the line of David firmly within the context of the families of man, the author now begins to mark off the line of the promise. The line of the promise is that elect nation through whom God intended to bring blessing and salvation to a lost world. He takes great pains to tell us that the nation is Israel, the descendants of the sons of Jacob.

1. *The family of Judah* (4:1-23). The list of the sons of Israel

begins with the family of Judah. According to the prophecy of his father Israel (Gen. 49:8-12), Judah was to be the leader of the families of Israel, and the promised blessing was to come to Israel and the nations through that family. With that promise in mind, the chronicler begins his enumeration of the household of Israel. The thought that the Davidic dynasty represents that chosen leadership is a central theme in the books of Chronicles. It should not go by without notice that the central themes of these books are being prepared in these opening genealogies. The stage is being set and the actors in the great drama to follow are given their proper introduction.

2. *The family of Simeon* (4:24-43). Simeon and his descendants come next in the list, probably because the family of Simeon shared the territory allotted to the family of Judah (Josh. 19:9).

3. *The families of the trans-Jordan: Reuben, Gad, the half-tribe of Manasseh* (5:1-26). The list of names is expanded to give a short history of the families that settled along the eastern banks of the Jordan. When the Israelites settled in the land of Canaan, three families remained on the east side of the Jordan, the families of Reuben, Gad, and half of the family of Manasseh (Num. 32; Josh. 13:8-33).

Reuben, the firstborn, had forfeited his birthright through immorality (Gen. 35:22; 49:4). Possession of the birthright meant preeminence among the families. The sons of Joseph, Ephraim and Manasseh, now enjoyed that privilege. In spite of that right of the firstborn, however, from the house of Judah, the family of David, was to come the true leader of the sons of Israel (1 Chron. 5:1-2).

What is the point of this short reminder of the early history of those families? The answer lies in one of the central themes of the books of Chronicles: God's grace, and His faithfulness to His promises. Throughout 1 and 2 Chronicles God's choice of David as king and the house of David as the channel of salvation is seen as an act of God's grace. Salvation is not a natural right that belongs to one from birth. Birthrights come and go. They are no guarantees of blessing. What ultimately matters is God's grace. The choice of Judah as the one from whom the Prince would come was based not on natural rights but on God's grace. David saw this clearly when he said: "Who am I, O LORD God, and what is my house that Thou hast brought me thus far? . . . Thou hast spoken of Thy servant's house for a great while to come, and hast regarded me according to the standard of a man of high degree, O LORD, God" (1 Chron. 17:16-17). Let the birthright go to whomever it belongs; the Prince will come from Judah.

Chapter 5 ends with another reminder of God's faithfulness (5:25-26). This time, however, the result is not salvation but judgment: the exile of the families of Reuben, Gad, and, the half-tribe of Manasseh. God's faithfulness cuts both ways. He is gracious and forgiving to those who put their trust in Him; but those who forsake Him to follow other gods He will punish. God stirred up the heart of the Assyrian king Tilgath-pilneser, and he carried the trans-Jordan into exile. When God did that, He was only acting out of faithfulness to His covenant with Israel. According to the covenant, trust would bring blessing, but disobedience would bring exile (Deut. 28).

The chronicler's emphasis on this last point runs parallel to the interest of his contemporary Daniel: "As it is written in the law of Moses, all this calamity has come on us; yet we have not sought the favor of the LORD our God by turning from our iniquity and giving attention to Thy truth. Therefore, the LORD has kept the calamity in store and brought it on us; for the LORD our God is righteous with respect to all His deeds which He has done, but we have not obeyed His voice" (Dan. 9:13-14).

4. *The family of Levi* (6:1-81). The list of the names of the family of Levi is carefully constructed. Its purpose is to make clear the line of descent of the priests and Levites.

The list begins with the levitical line that traces its descent from Aaron, the first priest (6:1-15). The chronicler begins with this line because only those Levites (descendants of Levi) who were descended from Aaron could legitimately do the work of a priest at the Temple (6:49; Num. 3:5-38) and could carry out the duties of the sacrificial system. The importance of that distinction is seen after the rebuilding of the Temple during the return from exile. If a priest could not establish that he was a descendant of Aaron, he could not serve in the new Temple as a priest (Neh. 7:63-65).

Why was the priesthood limited only to the descendants of Aaron? The priesthood stood in the pivotal position of mediating between God and man. It was by means of the duties of the priest that God's relationship to man was restored and maintained. Was the duty of the priest here being prescribed to Israel on the basis of a natural right? Does Israel's relationship to God rest on a birthright? The chronicler has not given explicit answers to those questions, although the overarching emphasis that he places on God's grace throughout these books suggests that, here also, God's grace, not inherited rights, lies at the base of man's relationship with God. The descendants of Aaron were priests because God chose them. They did not earn the right to mediate between God and Israel; God by grace gave them the right and the responsibility. The chronicler draws out the implications of that premise in verse 15 by ending the line of priests with the Exile into Babylon. The priesthood has meaning only when, by God's grace, the people dwell in the land.

The next section of the list of the descendants of Levi is a general enumeration of the levitical family (6:16-53). The purpose of this list may be seen from the descendants of Levi who are selected and emphasized: Samuel, Heman, Asaph, and Ethan. What do these "Levites" have in common? Elsewhere we know that these men and their descendants were the prophets who served God at the Temple (1 Sam. 3:21; 1 Chron. 25:1). They are the counterparts of the priests. Together with the priests, those prophets and their descendants maintained the relationship and fellowship between God and Israel at the Temple. Along with the Davidic king, those prophets and priests provided the basis of God's rule among His people; that is, they were the basis of the kingdom of God.

The chronicler's interest in the family of Levi includes not only the physical lineage of the descendants, but also the geographical borders of their inheritance (6:54-81). God's kingdom was a place as well as an exercise of power. God ruled within a realm, the land of promise. His rule, however, was not limited to that realm (2 Chron. 6:18).

5. *The remaining families of Israel* (7:1-44). The chronicler ends his genealogical and historical survey of the families of Israel by tracing briefly the descendants of Issachar, Benjamin, Naphtali, Manasseh, Ephraim, and Asher.

Two families are omitted from that list, the family of Dan (Gen. 30:1-6) and the family of Zebulun (Gen. 30:19-20). Those omissions are not without purpose. The writer is concerned to show that the house of Israel still consists of the twelve families of the sons of Jacob. Since he has counted the half-tribe of Manasseh as a complete family (1 Chron. 5:23-24) and has counted the Levites as part of the twelve families (1 Chron. 6:1-81), the omission of Dan and Zebulun is required to maintain the number twelve. By keeping the number at twelve families, he has said all he intends to say; that is, the whole house of Israel has a part in the plan of God to build His kingdom.

C. THE HOUSE OF SAUL (8:1—9:44)

The last list of names serves as a transition into the first narrative section, the death of Saul (1 Chron. 10:1-14). Continuing the genealogical style, the chronicler prepares the way for the opening of his narrative by giving the lineage of Israel's first king, Saul (1 Chron. 8:1-40). What does the last lists of names tell about Saul? For what purpose have those names been included? The answer lies in the way the lists of names are arranged in chapters 8 and 9. In both chapters, those "who lived in Jerusalem" (8:28; 9:34) are distinguished from those who lived in Gibeon (8:29; 9:35). The purpose of that distinction is to show that Saul was from that part of the family of Benjamin that is from Gibeon, not Jerusalem. There were Benjamites who lived in Jerusalem, but Saul was not of that group.

Those two cities, Gibeon and Jerusalem, were important centers. Jerusalem was the city of David. It was also Zion, the place where God's Temple had been built. It was the city where Israel met with God and was the center of all God's blessing and salvation (2 Chron. 6:6). Gibeon was where the Tabernacle of the Lord was kept. There, Zadok the high priest served the Lord and the musicians Heman and Jeduthun sang praises to the Lord accompanying the burnt offerings (1 Chron. 16:39-41). Gibeon was an important place of worship for Israel, and even Solomon went there on one occasion to worship (2 Chron. 1:3-6).

Gibeon, however, was not *God's* chosen place. Gibeon was chosen *by Israel* as the place where the Tabernacle could be kept. But God had chosen Jerusalem as the place where His name would dwell (2 Chron. 6:6). Not only was Jerusalem God's choice, but so was the house of David. Jerusalem and David are the two components of God's plan of salvation and blessing in the books of Chronicles; Saul and Gibeon are not.

By drawing the line connecting Gibeon and Saul, the way is prepared for the story of Saul to follow. Saul and Gibeon were chosen by Israel. Although God approved of both, neither succeeded in gaining a central place in His plan of salvation. As the contrast between David and Saul shows, God's plan must be carried out by God's people in God's way. God's way was David and Jerusalem.

D. THE DEATH OF SAUL (10:1-4).

Saul was Israel's first king. He was anointed by Samuel (1 Sam. 10:1) and fought valiantly against the Philistines and other enemies of God's people. Saul's kingship, however, ended in defeat as he proved to be a king not worthy to lead God's people (1 Sam. 13:13-14).

Because the house of Saul was not God's chosen instrument of salvation, the chronicler is interested only in the last and most significant event in Saul's reign as king: the defeat of Saul and his army by the Philistines at Gilboa. The account is almost a verbatim report of Saul's defeat in 1 Samuel 31.

Before we consider the account of Saul's death, it would be helpful to look first at more facts concerning Saul's life.

Along with David, Saul emerges from 1 Samuel as one of the dominant figures of that book. It seems to be without question that the writer's interest in Saul stems from the negative example set by this gallant but ungodly leader.

Almost from the start Saul's hopes for success as a leader of God's people appeared slight. In 1 Samuel 8 God's people, acting on impulse, decided to throw off their loyalties to God, their true king, and establish for themselves a king like the other nations (1 Samuel 8:7). Reluctantly, the prophet Samuel acceded to their wish and, according to God's instructions, set out to anoint a king for Israel. Saul, whose name meant "he who was requested," then provided a fitting, but tragic, reminder of the necessity to trust God for our salvation and not to set our eyes on our own strength.

Saul was humble (1 Sam. 9:21); he had stature among the people (1 Sam. 10:23-24); he was a gallant warrior (1 Sam. 11; 14:47-48); but Saul was not to be successful as Israel's king. He lacked the one feature that ultimately mattered: a heart for God. As God said through Samuel the prophet, "He has turned back from following Me, and has not carried out My commands" (1 Sam. 15:11).

As a candle burns brighter in darkness than in daylight, so David's rise to prominence in 1 Samuel was accomplished in the midnight of Saul's reign. Saul's deeds turned from bad to worse and David's successes became impossible to hide (1 Sam. 18:14-15). The final defeat of Saul at the hand of Israel's enemies was an outlandish reversal of the hopes that had come to settle on the shoulders of the Davidic king (e.g., Isa. 9:7). Far from shattering the enemies of God under his feet (cf. 2 Sam. 22:38-48), Saul's kingdom ended in the single act of falling to his knees upon his own sword (1 Sam. 31:4).

In a single moment of disobedience (1 Sam. 13:8-14) Saul's kingdom was destroyed. Unlike the chronicler, who devotes attention only to the final destruction of Saul's kingdom, the writer of 1 Samuel draws on every stage of the decline to show his lesson that obedience to the will of God is the bedrock of biblical leadership. From the single refusal to wait for the prophet Samuel before offering a sacrifice (1 Sam. 13:8-14), Saul's disobedient heart rebelled to the point of rejecting God's prophets and seeking help from the woman who was a medium at Endor (1 Sam. 28:6). The lesson of Saul's life is fittingly portrayed in Samuel's psalm to Saul:

> Has the LORD as much delight in burnt offerings and
>   sacrifice
> As in obeying the voice of the LORD?
> Behold, to obey is better than sacrifice,
> And to heed than the fat of rams.
> For rebellion is as the sin of divination,

And insubordination is as iniquity and idolatry.
Because you have rejected the word of the LORD,
He has also rejected you from being king.

1 Samuel 15:22-23

Therefore, we would miss the main point of 1 Samuel if we were to understand Saul's disobedient heart as merely the failure to do what God had requested.

The battle at Gilboa was a decisive battle in the war between Israel and the Philistines. What was at stake in the battle was nothing less than the control of Saul's kingdom. If Gilboa was lost, the Philistines would succeed in dividing the nation in half and controlling the major East-West trade route through Canaan. Although the details of the battle are not known, the Philistines did gain the upper hand, and Saul's army was defeated. Added to the account is an explanation of the cause of Saul's defeat: "So Saul died for his trespass which he committed against the LORD, because of the word of the LORD which he did not keep; and also because he asked counsel of a medium, making inquiry of it, and did not inquire of the LORD. Therefore He killed him, and turned the kingdom to David the son of Jesse" (1 Chron. 10:13-14).

That explanation assumes that we are familiar with the whole story of the reign of Saul given in 1 Samuel. When did Saul not keep the word of the Lord? When did Saul seek counsel from a medium? On two occasions, in the account in 1 Samuel, Saul did not keep the word of the Lord that was spoken through the prophet Samuel (1 Sam. 13:1-23 and 15:1-35). An important recurring lesson in the books of Samuel and the books of Chronicles is the importance of the leaders of God's people to follow the word of the Lord. Leadership is serious business. There is no room for only half obedience.

Saul also sought the counsel of a medium on one occasion (1 Sam. 28). Behind the condemnation of Saul for that act is the clear teaching of Scripture (Deut. 18:10-22). Israel was not to seek the will of God in the counsel of mediums or in the words of false prophets but in the word of God spoken by the prophets whom He had raised up. The centrality of the Word of God has always been the hallmark of godly leadership.

3

DAVID

II. DAVID (1 Chronicles 11:1—29:30)

David is a central figure in 1 and 2 Chronicles. The theme of salvation and blessing was personified in the reign of David over Israel. As a result, David became the standard by which all future kings were measured. A good king is one who does "according to all that his father David had done" (2 Chron. 29:2). Not only was David the standard for all the kings who followed him, but he was also the king who most epitomized the promised Messiah. For many of the biblical writers, to talk of David was to talk of the Messiah (e.g., Ezek. 34:23-24). Judging from some of his own psalms (e.g., Ps. 22), David even entertained that view about himself. Such a view of David seems also to have been the viewpoint of the chronicler. As he writes about David and evaluates later kings by the standards of David, he has in mind not just the David that was king, but also the "David" that would yet be king, the Messiah. It is in that sense that much of the perspective of the books of Chronicles is messianic. They look *forward* with anticipation to the coming King who will bring in God's final salvation and blessing.

The hope that is seen in the story of David is the same hope that finds its consolation in the words of the angel (Luke

2:10-11): "Behold, I bring you good news of a great joy which shall be for all the people; for today in the city of David there has been born for you a Savior, who is Christ the Lord."

Using the history of David and the Davidic kings, the chronicler weaves his hope for the future together with the evidence of God's faithfulness in the past and gives his readers a basis for trusting and obeying God in the present.

A. DAVID BECOMES KING OVER ISRAEL (11:1-3)

It was a foregone conclusion that David would be king. David's struggle to rise to power and the setback under the reign of Saul that loom so large in 1 Samuel are passed over, except for a simple comment from those who had gathered to make David king: "In times past, even when Saul was king, you were the one who led out and brought in Israel; and the LORD your God said to you, 'You shall shepherd My people Israel, and you shall be prince over My people Israel' " (1 Chron. 11:2).

It is because of verses like that that the chronicler has earned his reputation as being a first-rate man of words. In that one quotation he has embodied the essence of the whole of 1 Samuel: God has chosen David to be king, and God will bring to pass His will. That statement is not an idle observation from history; it is the basis of hope for the future. What God has promised, He will do. In that hope is echoed the thoughts of the prophet Isaiah, who also looked for the time when *the* Son of David would rule over God's Kingdom: "There will be no end to the increase of His government or of peace, on the throne of David and over his kingdom, to establish it and to uphold it with justice and righteousness from then on and forevermore. *The zeal of the LORD of hosts will accomplish this*" (Isa. 9:7, italics added). When the Messiah comes he will come like David—established by the mighty hand of God.

The account of David's anointing at Hebron contains only one addition to the account in 2 Samuel 5:1-3. In support of his emphasis on the power of God in bringing about His plans, the writer adds the comment that all that happened "according to the word of the LORD through Samuel" (v. 3). By the addition of that comment we see the real cause of David's anointing. David's kingship was a fulfillment of the words of Samuel the prophet. The events of Israel's history—the death of Saul, the reign of David and Solomon, and the downfall of the kingdom—were not merely the result of the political, economic, and social conditions of the day. They owed their cause to the acts of God in the history of His people. God was there working in the history of that people and in the lives of its leaders. As God worked, He revealed the meaning of that history to His prophets, so that when His words came to pass, the people could see the plan of God. This view toward the events is the same as that of the prophet Amos, "Surely the LORD God does nothing unless He reveals His secret counsel to His servants the prophets" (Amos 3:7).

In this section we see that David's kingship found confirmation in three important ways: (1) the consent of God's people (11:2-3); (2) the word of the prophet Samuel; and (3) the victories David receives from the hand of God.

B. THE CAPTURE OF JERUSALEM (11:4-8)

The account of David's capture of Jerusalem is brief. Despite the proud boasting of the Canaanite (Jebusite) occupants of the city, David was able to take the city because of the brave and resourceful men who gathered around him. Joab, who carried out the plan to capture Jerusalem, was made David's chief and commander. Archeologists suppose that David took the city by storming the low point of Jerusalem's walls and cutting off the city's water supply. The details of the capture here and in 2 Samuel, however, are not clear.

With David in possession of Jerusalem, the kingdom was given a centrally located capital with the best natural defenses in the area. Mount Zion, the city of David, became a citadel that symbolized God's eternal care and protection of His people. One Israelite songwriter put this into words that are still sung by God's people today:

> Great is the LORD, and greatly to be praised,
> In the city of our God, His holy mountain.
> Beautiful in elevation, the joy of the whole earth,
> Is Mount Zion in the far north,
> The city of the great King.
> God, in her palaces,
> Has made Himself known as a stronghold."

> Ps. 48:1-3

C. DAVID'S MIGHTY MEN (11:9-12:40)

A man is known by the company he keeps. That is the idea behind the enumeration of the mighty men who surrounded David and aided his establishment of the kingship. The chronicler has already described the mighty deed of David's commander, Joab. Now he turns to describe David's army. The list of mighty men is given in three sections: the chiefs among David's men (11:10-25); the mighty men in David's army (11:26-47); and the mighty men who joined David at Ziklag, while he was still fleeing Saul (12:1-40).

The point of the detailed enumeration of the names and exploits of those men is to show that David was a leader who had gained the full confidence and support of the best men in Israel. Those were men who had received the medal of honor in service to David and his kingdom.

The chronicler has selected an interesting episode that serves to demonstrate why David attracted the loyalty of those men (11:15-19). When three men, at the risk of their own lives, broke through enemy lines to draw water from a well for David, David showed remarkable sensitivity to the dangers his men faced in battle. Pouring the water out as an offering to the Lord, David said, "Be it far from me before God that I should do this. Shall I drink the blood of these men who went at the risk of their lives? For at the risk of their lives they brought it" (11:19).

David is portrayed as a leader who cares sincerely for those entrusted to his care. David is like the Russian general in Alexander Solzhenitsyn's novel *August 1914*. The general, Samsonov, preferred to plan military operations with big maps. He would say, "If the maps were big enough to make it difficult to draw arrows, you were more likely to remember how hard it was for the troops to cover the same distances on the ground." Such leadership inspires confidence.

The list of mighty men who came to David at Ziklag is given only in 1 Chronicles (12:1-40). There are several points that seem to be emphasized by the inclusion of that list. First, the men who joined David and supported his kingship were from "all Israel." Men from every family in Israel joined with David. Second, the number of the men who joined David is given close attention. The number of men following David from all Israel was very large. "There was a great army like the army of God" (12:22). Third, the large number of men that had joined David represented an even larger group of kinsmen who had stayed behind but had given their full support to those who went to join David (12:39-40). Indeed, there was great joy in Israel over the leadership of David and over the support that the people expressed for David. Fourth, even the kinsmen of Saul from the family of Benjamin came out to join David (1 Chron. 12:2, 16, 29). Fifth, the support given to David by that great army of mighty men was not merely military assistance. The chronicler states explicitly why those men joined David: "to turn the kingdom of Saul to him, according to the word of the LORD" (12:23). The response of those mighty men shows that God was at work fulfilling the word He had spoken about David by the prophet Samuel (1 Sam. 16:12).

That list of mighty men in 1 Chronicles 12 reveals the great popular enthusiasm for David. This was not a new popularity, for David had the same grass roots support even when he was fleeing from Saul. Now that Saul was gone, God's choice also became the choice of the people. All the people were of one mind to make David king (1 Chron. 12:38).

To show the character of the popular support given to David by those mighty men, the chronicler has included a short song which some of the people sang as they came to David:

> We are yours, O David,
> And with you, O son of Jesse!
> Peace, peace to you,
> And peace to him who helps you;
> Indeed, your God helps you!
>
> 1 Chron. 12:18

That simple song says a great deal about the character of the people's support for the kingship of David. With David there was peace (*shalom*); and with those who helped David there was peace (*shalom*) because God was David's helper! Those thoughts about David and his kingship are not far from what is said about the Son of David, called Immanuel in Isaiah: He shall be called the "Prince of Peace [*Shalom*]" (9:6).

D. DAVID AND THE ARK OF THE COVENANT (13:1—16:43)

The Ark of the Covenant plays a central role in these chapters. The Ark was a wooden chest overlaid with gold. It was handcrafted by Israelite artisans during the period of wilderness wanderings. The pattern for building the Ark was given to Moses at Mount Sinai, and it became one of the most important components of Israel's worship (Ex. 25:9-22). By means of the Ark, the invisible presence of the God of the

Covenant was visualized. The Ark was no mere symbol of God's presence. It was the place where God had chosen to center His presence among His people (Ex. 25:22).

The chronicler's concern with the whereabouts of the Ark during the reign of David is a reflection of the importance the Ark of the Covenant held for Israel. The first official duties of David in 1 Chronicles concern the care for the Ark. The Ark had been captured by the Philistines (1 Sam. 4:11), but had subsequently been returned to Israel and was being kept in the house of Abinadab in the city of Kiriath-jearim (1 Sam. 7:1).

David's desire to bring the Ark to Jerusalem to be near the center of God's people shows his concern for God's presence to be with His people and in His Kingdom. David had taken seriously the promise of the covenant God to dwell among His people (Ex. 19:3-6; 25:8). He also had seen the need of the people to reestablish their relationship with God. They had not sought the Ark of God in the days of Saul (1 Chron. 13:3), and David's concern was that God's people again seek the Lord at the Ark, which meant to come before God at the Ark and pray (2 Chron. 6:19-21).

The account of the movement of the Ark to Jerusalem is given in stages. Each stage of the process contributes to the lesson intended for the reader.

1. *Removing the Ark from Kiriath-jearim* (13:1-14). The first stage of the description of David's moving the Ark to Jerusalem teaches an awesome lesson. The lesson is the seriousness and reality of God's holy presence. The presence of the holy God among His people was not, and is not, to be taken lightly. God had graciously promised to be near His people; that is, in their very midst. His presence was real and not to be treated as merely symbolic. God's holiness can never be treated with mere empty ritualism.

In the books of Moses (Genesis to Deuteronomy), God had

instructed Israel how to respond appropriately to His presence (Ex. 25-31). Much of that instruction consisted in performing special acts at special times and places. There was always the danger that by performing those actions an empty ritual would replace a true respect for God's presence. The chronicler, like many of the prophets, is particularly concerned to warn the people against taking those sacred actions and holy objects lightly. In chapter 13, the account of the removing of the Ark from Kiriath-jearim is one such warning.

All Israel went with David to Kiriath-jearim to get the Ark and bring it to Jerusalem (1 Chron. 13:6). The chronicler reminds the reader that the Ark was the Ark of God, "who is enthroned above the cherubim, where His name is called" (13:6).

There was much celebration before the Ark as David and the people moved it along the hilly roadways to Jerusalem: "And David and all Israel were celebrating before God with all their might, even with songs and with lyres, harps, tambourines, cymbals, and with trumpets" (13:8). However, all was not well. God's Word was not obeyed. The joy was there, the excitement was there, the music and celebration were great, but God's presence was not being properly acknowledged. All the music and singing was a hollow substitute for an attitude of deep respect for the presence of God. The people had carried the Ark of God on a cart pulled by oxen (13:7, 9). That may have been a way suitable for the Philistines to carry the Ark (1 Sam. 6:7), but God had instructed Israel to carry it in a very specific and quite different manner: the Levites (sons of Kohath) were to carry the Ark with the "carrying poles" inserted in the rings on either side of the Ark, so that no one would "touch the holy objects and die" (Num. 4:15).

It was the failure to be faithful in that little matter that led to the great tragedy in 1 Chronicles 13:9-10: "When they came to the threshing floor of Chidon, Uzza put out his hand to hold the ark, because the oxen nearly upset it. And the anger of the LORD burned against Uzza, so He struck him down because he put out his hand to the ark; and he died there before God.''

That event took its sudden, tragic turn very unexpectedly while the people were rejoicing over the return of the Ark. Things happened so unexpectedly that David responded in anger and fear, not knowing whether to carry on or to postpone the moving of the Ark. Having decided out of apparent desperation to postpone any further moving of the Ark, David left it at the home of Obed-edom, along the way to Jerusalem.

Almost as suddenly as it had come, the perplexing tragedy of this account ended. The story concludes with one of the central themes of salvation in the books of Chronicles: the blessing of the Lord. ''Thus the ark of God remained with the family of Obed-edom in his house three months; and the LORD blessed the family of Obed-edom with all that he had'' (13:14).

The first stage of the transfer of the Ark to Jerusalem was marked by both tragedy and joy. If God's people lose sight of who He is, even for a moment, the consequence can be tragic. Taking God's word seriously in faith and obedience is the remedy for neglect. David and all Israel had failed to carry the Ark in the right way. They had neglected the proper ritual (1 Chron. 15:13), and that had led to an empty ritualism. They had shown great interest in the celebration of song and music. They were apparently making a great display of their moving the Ark. All of that was good, but it did not take the place of an inward attitude acknowledging the presence of a holy God in their midst.

2. *Restoring fellowship with God* (14:1-17). Not only had the Lord restored the blessing of His presence at the Ark in the house of Obed-edom (1 Chron. 13:14), but David's kingdom

also was again experiencing God's blessing. The chronicler singles out three events from David's life to show that the Lord had blessed his kingdom. These events in chapter 14 are to be read as a direct consequence of David's taking proper care for the Ark of God. The point in this section is to show that blessing from God follows obedience to God's word.

First, the chronicler recounts the tribute paid to David by the surrounding nations. Hiram, king of Tyre, sent messengers bearing materials and workmen who were to build a house for David. To David that was a sign that the Lord was establishing David's kingdom (14:1-2). The Lord had made David's house great.

Second, the chronicler takes up the theme of David's sons and daughters (14:3-7). In a manner reminiscent of the godly men in the early chapters of Genesis, the writer shows God's blessing on David by the enumeration of the births of his children. We can almost hear the words of Genesis echoing in the account of David's family: "And God blessed them; and God said to them, 'Be fruitful and multiply' " (Gen. 1:28).

The third sign of God's blessing is David's victory over the enemies of God's people, the Philistines (14:8-17). The Philistines heard that David had been anointed king over all Israel. Since the defeat of Saul at Gilboa (1 Chron. 10:1-14), the Philistines had controlled the major lines of communication and trade throughout the land of Israel. A united kingdom under David again meant a major threat to the Philistines' rule. Responding quickly to the news, the Philistines engaged David in combat by sending a raiding party out against him in the Valley of Rephaim, just southwest of Jerusalem. By the hand of the Lord, David defeated the Philistines and "the fame of David went out into all the lands; and the LORD brought the fear of him on all the nations" (14:17).

The events of chapters 13 and 14 are memorialized by renaming the locality where they occurred. The site of the

tragic death of Uzza is named "Perez-uzza" (breakthrough
of Uzza) because there the Lord "broke through" (*paraz*)
against Uzza (1 Chron. 13:11). The site of the defeat of the
Philistines was named "Baal-perazim" (master of breakthrough) because there God "broke through" (*paraz*) the
enemy as "the breakthrough (*perez*) of waters" (14:11). In
both events the names emphasize God's breaking in upon the
lives of His people for salvation or judgment. The God of the
Bible is the living God. When He acts for His people in salvation or against them in judgment, His presence is felt with all
the power and presence of the breaking through (*paraz*) of a
wall of water in the bursting of a dam. In the light of David's
restored relationship to God, the chronicler goes on to recount the moving of the Ark into Jerusalem (chap. 15).

In the account of the Ark, two things are emphasized—
God's presence and God's power. Both must be taken
seriously if one is to reckon with the living God.

There is an overall purpose in the chronicler's stressing just
those two points in connection with the Ark of the Covenant.
As will be seen later (2 Chron. 6:1-42), the central importance
of the Ark of the Covenant for Israel was that it marked the
point of prayer and communion between God and Israel. It is
those two features—God's presence and God's power—that
give sense to prayer and make it effective. The chronicler,
then, is laying serious theological groundwork in these
chapters by stressing the importance of obedience in fellowship and the importance of God's presence and power in
prayer.

3. *The Ark rests in Jerusalem* (15:1—16:43). With the events
of 1 Chronicles 13 and 14, David had learned many important
lessons. He now returned to his original intentions of moving
the Ark to Jerusalem and restoring the presence of God to its
rightful place—in the midst of God's people. The important
points of chapters 15 and 16 will be: (1) the centrality of the

priests and the Levites; (2) the joy of God's presence; and (3) the concern that the worship of God might not be confined to one people and one nation, but that all nations and all peoples might look to God as their Savior and Lord.

a. The centrality of the priests and the Levites (15:1-15). David had learned that the proper way to approach God in fellowship and worship was in the manner prescribed by God Himself. He prepared a place for the Ark of God and there set up a tent (15:1). David was following the instruction that God gave to Moses at Mount Sinai (Ex. 26:7ff). He then commanded that only the Levites were to carry the Ark, and that they were to carry it in the prescribed way (15:2-15). The importance of that point is shown by the detail supplied in these verses. To show that his heart was in the right place, David carried out God's will to the letter. The key phrases here are "according to the ordinance" (v. 13) and "as Moses had commanded according to the word of the Lord" (v. 15). All this concern for the exactness of the procedure was not an empty formalism; it was a desire to please God and worship Him in reverence that overflows into action. David had learned the lesson that in worship, as well as in life, actions can speak as loud as words.

All the emphasis, however, is not put on David's actions. Worship is more than a prescribed set of activities carried out to the letter; worship is also an expression. That lesson is drawn from the report of David's preparation for music and praise.

b. The joy of God's presence (15:16—16:6). The description of David's preparation for worship in 1 Chronicles 15:16-29 clearly shows the extent of joy and praise he intended for his newly established center for worship. In today's categories, David was providing a full orchestra and choir.

Whatever kind of worship service we might be accustomed to today, it seems certain that the form of worship established by David was marked by much singing and playing of musical instruments. If we can judge by those preparations and the many musical references in the book of Psalms, music and praise were the two fundamental features of Israel's worship. Worship was the singing of God's praises before the congregation. What better description of worship could be given than that in 1 Chronicles 15:16—"to raise sounds of joy"?

In the report of David's moving the Ark into Jerusalem, one verse stands negatively against the sounds of joy and praise that mark the time of celebration: "And it happened when the ark of the covenant of the LORD came to the city of David, that Michal the daughter of Saul looked out of the window, and saw King David leaping and making merry; and she despised him in her heart" (1 Chron. 15:29).

c. "Tell of His glory among the nations" (16:7-43). As part of the joy of worshiping in God's presence, a hymn was sung the day of dedication of the Ark (16:8-36). It is likely that there were many hymns sung during that time of joy and dedication, but the hymn included here was chosen because it most clearly portrays the thoughts and hopes of the people as they gathered to inaugurate that new phase in their relationship with God.

At the heart of Israel's call to be the people of God lies the purpose of God expressed in Genesis 12:3: "In you all the families of the earth shall be blessed." The hymn is, in fact, a medley of hymns from the book of Psalms and is so arranged to give emphasis to one central idea: the intended result of Israel's worship of God was the salvation of the nations so that they, too, might worship God at His Temple. Israel's worship was evangelical: it was to include all people of all lands.

Zechariah, also a prophet to the post-exilic community, showed the same hope and understanding: "Sing for joy and be glad, O daughter of Zion; for behold I am coming and I will dwell in your midst,'' declares the LORD. ''And many nations will join themselves to the LORD in that day and will become My people. Then I will dwell in your midst, and you will know that the LORD of hosts has sent Me to you'' (Zech. 2:10-11).

A summary of the hymn will bring out the main lines of that theme.

The hymn begins, as most hymns, with a call to worship (16:8-13). It is especially striking that the hymn turns almost immediately to the theme of the nations' (Gentiles) participation in that worship: ''Make known His deeds among the peoples'' (v. 8*b*). The terminology used in verse 8 calls to mind the kind of worship seen in the stories of Abraham where, having built an altar in the land of Canaan among its inhabitants, he ''called upon the name of the LORD'' (Gen. 12:8). Also the prophet Isaiah reminds the people of Israel that when the Holy One of Israel is in their midst, they will say: ''Give thanks to the LORD, call on His name. Make known His deeds among the peoples; make them remember that His name is exalted'' (Isa. 12:4).

After the call to worship, the hymn extols the greatness and the grace of God (16:14-22). The theme of God's grace is recalled in the remembrance of His covenant with Abraham. When Israel was only a small family moving from nation to nation, God promised to give them the land of Canaan and protected them among the nations: ''and He reproved kings for their sakes, saying, 'Do not touch My anointed ones, and do My prophets no harm' '' (16:21*b*-22).

After a renewed call to worship (16:23-24), the hymn extols the greatness of God over the vain idols of the nations (16:25-26) and recalls the power and glory of God, the Creator (16:27-30).

The hymn ends with a call to all creation to turn to the Lord in trust and obedience, because He is coming in judgment as well as salvation (16:31-36).

It is very significant for the message of the chronicler that he recounts this hymn as the exemplary hymn of the dedication of the Ark. He shows that in David's day, Israel's worship was directed *outward* towards the nations as well as *upward* toward God, as it had been in the time of Abraham and would be in the days of the Messiah according to the prophet Isaiah (Isa. 12:1-6).

4

DAVID AND THE PROMISE—
THE FIRST ACCOUNT

E. DAVID AND THE PROMISE (17:1—29:30)

In these chapters we find the single most important event in the life of David—God's covenant promise to give him an eternal kingdom. By sheer repetition (three times), the point is made clear that the house of David is God's chosen vehicle for bringing salvation to the nations. The Messiah will be a son of David. Much like David's own immediate son Solomon, the coming One will be a man of peace (*shalom*), and in His day God's people will have rest.

1. *The first account of God's promise to David* (17:1—21:30). There are several important components to the promise that God makes to David in these chapters. In some respects the promises relate to David and his own rule over Israel. In other respects, however, the promises concern a specific descendant of David, the Messiah, who will do for Israel far more than even his father David. In this first account of the promise (Davidic covenant), the focus is clearly on those features of the promises that relate to David. The chronicler's concern is to throw light on the fulfillment of the specific promises to David in his own lifetime. By showing God's

faithfulness in His promises to David, he is giving a basis for trust in God's faithfulness concerning that descendant of David, the Messiah, who is in the center of the message of hope.

First Chronicles 17:8-9 helps to show the outline that follows the first account. In 17:8, God promises to give victory to David from all his enemies, so the account of David's victories is recorded in chapters 18-20. In 17:9, God promises that through David He will establish a *place* for His people, Israel. As the following verses and Deuteronomy 12:1-11 make clear, the Lord has in mind primarily a place for His Temple. Thus, in chapter 21, we find the events leading up to the selection of the site for the Temple—the threshing floor of Ornan.

a. The promise (17:1-15). When David determined to build God a permanent house (Temple), his plans had to undergo some modification. David could not build the house; David's descendant, a later king, would build the house. What was so wrong with David? Why could he not build the Temple? The answer comes from God's reply to David's plan: "I have never had need of a house in which to dwell. From the earliest times a simple tent for my dwelling has been all I asked for. Did I ever ask any of my leaders to make me a permanent house? When I want a house *I'll choose* who will build it for me" (1 Chron. 17:5-6, author's paraphrase). In other words, as Moses had said much earlier in Deuteronomy 12:5, God alone must choose the place for His dwelling. The freedom of God to choose His dwelling place was not negotiable. God's purpose among His people was a sovereign and gracious gift. It could not be taken for granted or be manipulated or prearranged. In every detail, down to the very one who was to build the house, God's will, not man's, was to be the determining factor. In a later passage (1 Chron. 22:8) the further reason behind God's rejection of David is given as well.

After rejecting David's plan to build the Temple, God announced His own plan (17:11-15): a son of David, a Davidic king whom God Himself would choose, would build God's house, the Temple. When this son came, he would not only build God's house, he would be ruler of a kingdom established by God forever—God's eternal kingdom.

To see the importance of this promise it is necessary to contrast this passage with 2 Samuel 7:1-17. In that account, the author is interested in the Messiah who will rule over God's eternal kingdom, but he is also interested in the short-range implications of God's promise. He is interested in David's immediate descendants, especially Solomon. How does Solomon fit into that promise? Solomon was a descendant of David, he built the Temple, and was a man of peace. To what extent does Solomon figure in this promise of an eternal King to follow David? The remainder of 2 Samuel and the book of Kings is an attempt to answer that question. The answer is that the immediate descendants of David, Solomon through the last king before the Exile, Zedekiah, did not fulfill the promise. Had the promise rested in them alone, Israel's hope would have led to despair. The author of 2 Samuel prepared his readers for that inevitable conclusion by including the words of God to David, "When he commits iniquity I will correct him with the rod of men and the strokes of the sons of men" (2 Sam. 7:14*b*). Those words clearly show that the immediate descendants of David would not measure up to the standards of the One ultimately envisioned in that promise. As God later makes clear, the promise to David had attached to it the obligation of obedience: "Now the word of the LORD came to Solomon saying, "Concerning this house which you are building, *if* you walk in My statutes and execute My ordinances and keep all My commandments by walking in them, then I will carry out My word *with you* which I spoke to David your father" (1 Kings 6:11-12, italics added). Prophets like Isaiah made it very clear that, in spite of the failure of the descendants of David, God's promise would still be fulfilled in the son of David who was to come: "And His name will be called Wonderful Counselor, Mighty God, Eternal Father, Prince of Peace. There will be no end to the increase of His government or of peace, on the throne of David and over his kingdom, to establish it and to uphold it with justice and righteousness from then on and forevermore" (9:6).

It is from that perspective of hope that the chronicler draws out the significance of God's promise to David—not over-looking the role of Solomon and the other Davidic kings in that promise, but looking beyond them to the future fulfill-ment. The chronicler has his mind set, not on the disobedient Davidic kings that led his people to exile, but on Him who said "my food is to do the will of Him who sent Me, and to accomplish His work" (John 4:34).

b. David's response (17:16-27). In David's response to God's promise, two qualities of his heart are apparent: humility, and trust in God. His first response was, "Who am I, O LORD God, and what is my house that Thou has brought me this far?" (17:16). But having considered what God had just promised, David went on to say that his rise from a shepherd to a king was a very small thing compared to the high status God had now bestowed upon him. What God had now promised regarding the One to come was beyond any of David's expectations, and he realized that its fulfillment was beyond his own powers: "What glory can David add to that which you, O Lord, have chosen to do with your servant?" (v. 16, author's paraphrase).

Flowing naturally out of that realization of his own power-lessness, David's prayer turned to the praise of Israel's redeemer and his confidence in God to accomplish what He has promised (17:20-27). What better way was there for the chronicler to reaffirm Israel's hope and trust in the coming Deliverer than to recount for his readers the trust and con-fidence with which David responded to the promise of His coming? David's response must surely have been the only proper one: "What more can David still say to Thee? . . . O LORD, for Thy servant's sake, and according to Thine own heart, Thou has wrought all this greatness, to make known all these great things" (17:18-19).

c. The defeat of the enemy (18:1—20:8). With a broad brush and occasional detail, the chronicler paints a vivid picture of David's military victories. The theme of these chapters is stated twice: "And the LORD helped David wherever he went" (18:6*b*, 13*b*). That is contrasted with the statement "The Arameans were not willing to help the sons of Ammon anymore" (19:19). The lesson of that collage of warfare is the same as that celebrated in Psalm 2: the kings of the earth can devise only an empty plan against the Lord and His Anointed (Ps. 2:1-2). As He had promised (1 Chron. 17:8), God was with David and delivered him from all his enemies and made a great name for David among all the people of the land. This is historical evidence that God would also give strength and victory to His Messiah, the Son of David. In a systematic plan of battle, David delivered the fatal blow to Israel's enemies: the Philistines (1 Chron. 18:1), the Moabites (18:2), the Arameans (18:3-11), the Edomites (18:12-13), and the Ammonites (19:1—20:3). In chapter 19, David's wars are not viewed as wars of aggression, for it was necessary that he defend himself against humiliating acts of aggression by his enemies against him (19:7).

From a historical perspective, these chapters show that David acted quickly and decisively to rid his kingdom of internal oppression and threat of foreign invasion. By setting up garrisons in the states surrounding Israel (18:6, 13), David extended his rule far beyond his own territorial boundaries. The growth of the nation Israel had paralleled that of its king, who had been a lone shepherd boy, but was now a leader of nations (1 Chron. 17:7).

d. "I will establish a place" (21:1-30). Having demonstrated the fulfillment of God's promise to David that He would cut off his enemies from before him, the chronicler recounts the fulfillment of the second portion of God's promise to David: "I will appoint a place for My people Israel" (1 Chron. 17:9). Certainly the Lord meant that He would make Israel's land secure and that the people would live in peace. However, the words of God are referring not merely to a place to dwell, but *the place* where God Himself would dwell, namely the Temple whose site was chosen by the Lord Himself (chapter 21). That the Temple is preeminently in view in God's promise in 1 Chronicles 17:9 can be seen in the verses that follow. The central task of the promised descendant is that he should build a Temple for the Lord (1 Chron. 17:12).

God's choice of the Temple site, however, was carried out through the instrumentality of His servant David. The occasion of the selection of the Temple site is recorded in great detail, because the events point out in remarkable clarity the ultimate purpose for the Temple: God's salvation for His people.

David had angered God by numbering his army (21:1-7). That was apparently a reflection of David's lack of trust in God to save His people. Although David confessed his sin, he was required to bear the consequences of that sin (21:8-12). David's reply to the prophet Gad provides the thematic statement of the narrative: "Let me fall into the hand of the LORD, for His mercies are very great" (21:13). After thousands fell by the plague that the Lord had sent upon His people, He was grieved and called His messenger of destruction to a halt (21:15). At the site where the messenger halted, the threshing floor of Ornan the Jebusite, David fell down before the Lord and pled to let the punishment fall upon him and his house rather than the people (21:16-17). But God commanded David to build an altar on that site and offer up the sacrifice He had provided in His law. That site was where God had chosen to build His house (21:18—22:1). In a very dramatic and climactic way, the purpose of the building of the Temple was given. It was not to be a religious shrine, but the place where sinful man would meet with a righteous and holy God—where God would genuinely show that His mercies were great.

In 1 Chronicles 21:1 the Hebrew word *satan* (without the definite article) means simply "adversary." It is a common word in the historical books to describe the enemies of Israel (1 Sam. 29:4; 2 Sam. 19:23; 1 Kings 5:4; 11:9-14, 23, 25). The text appears to be suggesting that a new uprising of Israel's enemies had precipitated David's move to number his army. That seems to be borne out by verse 12, which mentions the impending threat of Israel's enemies, and by the parallel passage in 2 Samuel 24:1-25 which connects David's numbering, his army with the anger of the Lord that burned against Israel. The association of an attack from external enemies and the anger of the Lord is not immediately clear until it is noted that, for the biblical historians, the Lord's anger against Israel commonly resulted in oppression from her enemies.

> And *the anger of the Lord burned against Israel,* and He gave them into the hands of plunderers who plundered them; and He sold them into the hands of their enemies around them, so that they could no longer stand before their enemies. [Judg. 2:14, italics added; see also 2:20; 3:8; 10:7; 2 Kings 13:3; 23:26].

This passage, then, should be read as a commentary on 2 Samuel 24 and on *satan,* the Hebrew word for adversary.

5

DAVID AND THE PROMISE—
THE SECOND ACCOUNT

2. *The second account of God's promise to David* (22:1—
27:34). In the first account of God's promise to David
(1 Chron. 17:1—21:30), we saw God's faithfulness to His
promise by what He had accomplished through those aspects
of the promise that specifically concerned David. In the second account of the promise to David, we will see how David
himself made preparations for the fulfillment of those aspects
of the promise that extended beyond his own reign. David
prepared for the future fulfillment of the promise, and he did
so in very concrete, specific terms: he gathered the material
for building the Temple (22:1-19) and appointed the officials
who would administer the kingdom after him (23:1—27:34).

Embodied in David's zealous activity in these chapters is an
important lesson: the preoccupation of God's people with the
hope of God's promise. David showed by his actions that his
uppermost desire was to see God's promise fulfilled. The
focus of the promise was the building of the house of God.
David did not rest until all the provisions for building the
house had been made. The picture of David given in these
chapters aptly depicts David's own expression of his desire to
care for the Temple in Psalm 69:9: "Zeal for Thy house has
consumed me." In the chronicler's day, the post-exilic

period, God's people were in need of stirring up. Judging from the words of the prophets of that period (e.g., Haggai 1:2), the people and their leaders had little of the zeal for the promises of God shown by David in these chapters. Their hope had waned, and the prophets were called to stir up their hearts to act in trust that God would prove faithful to His promise (cf. Haggai 2:20-23). God's people in the past have always acted in faith on the promises of God, for the hope of the believer is the faithfulness of God.

a. Preparations for the Temple building (22:1-19). This section does not have a parallel in the other historical books. The chronicler, drawing on his own sources of information (perhaps royal records), shows that David was responsible for gathering the building materials and workers (22:1-4, 14-19) and for ensuring that the Temple plans corresponded to the promise of God (22:5-13).

By including the charge of David to Solomon, the chronicler has added to the reasons David himself was not to build the Temple. The Temple was to be built by a man of peace, not by one who had shed much blood (22:8). Therefore his son Solomon, a man of peace (*shalom*), was to build the Temple.

But, in David's charge to Solomon an even more important qualification to God's promise is given: obedience to the will of God (22:13). The right to be God's leader demands the responsibility to be obedient to His will. Only then will the king prosper. As the chronicler and the biblical historians are quick to point out, even Solomon, a man of great wisdom and understanding, would not measure up to that qualification (1 Kings 11:1-13). In fact, after the chronicler has written his final sentence (2 Chron. 36:23), still occupying the center of attention is the question: Who will be the one to build the Lord's Temple? Apart from the New Testament, that question remains unanswered, even today.

b. The administration of the Temple and the kingdom
(23:1—27:34). First Chronicles 23:1-2 provides the outline for
the remaining chapters of 1 Chronicles: "Now when David
reached old age, he made his son Solomon king over Israel.
And he gathered together [organized] all the leaders of Israel
with the priests and the Levites." In reverse order, that summary is the basis for the account of David's organization of
the Levites (23:1-32; 24:20-31), the priests (24:1-19), the musicians and doorkeepers (25:1—26:32), and the princes of Israel
(27:1-34). The enthronement of Solomon, noted first in this
passage, is the concern of the third account of the promise to
David (28:1—29:30).

•The organization of the Levites (23:3-32). David did not
originate the special status of the Levites among the families
of Israel, nor did he for the first time appoint them as servants in the worship of God. That was done by God through
Moses on Mount Sinai (Num. 3). However, David was alert
to the will of God and had planned that the Temple be ad-
ministered according to it.

The arrangement of chapter 23 is simple and straightforward. The names of the heads of the family of Levi are
listed (23:3-24), and then the duties specified by David are
enumerated (23:25-32).

The family of Levites was divided into three major groups:
the sons of Gershon (23:7-11); the sons of Kohath (23:12-20);
and the sons of Merari (23:21-23).

Their duties included all the work of the Temple worship,
with the exception of the work only a priest (a son of Aaron)
could do. Previously, the major task of the Levites had been
to carry the parts and utensils of the Tabernacle (cf. Num.
3:1—4:49). But now that the Lord had established peace for
Israel through David and had chosen to dwell in Jerusalem,
the work of the Levites was reduced to that of caring for the
Temple, which was to be built by David's descendant
(23:28-32).

•The organization of the priests (24:1-19). Because the

work of the priests (sons of Aaron) has been mentioned in connection with the duties of the Levites (23:28), the subject of the duties of the priests is briefly mentioned as well in this chapter. At the conclusion of chapter 24 is an enumeration of the Levite family (24:20-31).

The priesthood in Israel could be carried out only by a descendant of the house of Aaron (Num. 18:7). The duty of the priest was to attend to the altar and to perform service "inside the veil," that is, within the Temple itself (cf. Num. 18:1-7). The point of the list is to show that David, with the priests Zadok and Ahimelech, had organized the work of the priests into groups of twenty-four. Each group of priests was to carry out the service of worship for one week (2 Chron. 23:8).

• The remaining Levites (24:20-31). This list is not merely an appendix to the earlier list of Levites. Here the order of service is enumerated as it had been determined by the casting of lots. No detail in the arrangement of the Temple worship was considered unimportant by David. Although for many these passages are not exciting reading, they do give a very insightful glimpse into the heart of David the king. Like a mother planning the wedding of an only child, David gave every detail his full time and attention.

• The organization of the musicians (25:1-31). It is clear from the genealogies that Asaph (1 Chron. 6:39-43), Heman (1 Chron. 6:33), and Jeduthun (Ethan) (1 Chron. 6:44-47) were Levites. Each came from one of the three chief families: Gershon, Kohath, and Merari. David also was responsible for organizing their families into the orders of Temple musicians. Their responsibilities are described as "prophesying with lyres, harps, and cymbals" (25:1), which in that day was a way of saying "singing praises to God." Praise and worship at the Temple were accompanied by musical instruments. The chronicler is interested in tracing the origins of this service back to David.

• The organization of the Levitical officials (26:1-32). The account of David's organization of the Levites is concluded by summary of the duties of three further groups of Levites: the gatekeepers (26:1-19); the treasury guards (1 Chron. 26:20-28); and the ministers of external affairs (26:29-32).

The gatekeepers were the Temple guards. It is carefully noted that David had wisely selected those men from families whose leaders were capable men, able to do the job (26:8). Just as it was important to assign musicians to lead the worship and praise (1 Chron. 25:7), so also it was important to find "valiant men" (warriors) to guard the gate (26:7).

The writer's concern for the details of David's organization led him to include even the number of guards at each of the gates around the Temple (26:17-18). Because the King James translators did not translate the rare Persian word *parbar* in verse 18, the tally of guards at the west gate long was rendered by the senseless "At Parbar westward, four at the causeway, and two at Parbar" (KJV). Although the meaning is still far from certain, the sense seems to be: "For the western courtyard: four guards on the road and two in the courtyard" (author's translation). The point of the passage is that David organized a well-guarded Temple with twenty-four guardposts manned day and night. That need for security at the Temple is understandable, not only in light of the value of the Temple building itself, but also in light of the treasures stored in its treasury (26:27-28).

•The organization of the princes of Israel (27:1-34). The account of David's organization and preparation concludes with a list of his army (27:1-15); tribal leaders (27:16-24); administrators (27:25-31); and counselors (27:32-34).

6

DAVID AND THE PROMISE—
THE THIRD ACCOUNT

3. *The third account of God's promise to David* (28:1—
29:30). The chronicler's primary concern in recounting
events in the life of David has been the promise of a coming
King to reign over God's people. God made a promise to
David that one of his descendants would rule over His
kingdom and build a house for Him. In the chronicler's own
day the promise had still not been fulfilled. His emphasis on
the promise of God is seen in his repeating the account of the
promise three times. In the first account, he told of the announcement of the promise to David (1 Chron. 17:1-27). In
the second account, the announcement of the promise is made
to Solomon (1 Chron. 22:1-19). Now, for a third time, the
promise is recounted to be announced to a congregation of
the leaders of Israel (28:1).

In this third account, as in the second (1 Chron. 22:7-13),
Solomon is taken to be the descendant of the promise by virtue of his being a man of peace and his building the Temple.
From David's perspective there seemed little doubt that God's
promise was about to be fulfilled in the reign of Solomon
(28:5-7). Certainly the preparations made for the building of
the Temple showed that David had little doubt that Solomon

was the one. He even said of Solomon's kingdom that the
Lord "will establish his kingdom forever" if he was obedient
to the will of God (28:7). The crucial factor in David's expectation seems to have been the qualification of obedience. If
the chronicler is still waiting in hope for the fulfillment of the
promise to David, then he, contrary to David, certainly does
not believe Solomon was the son promised. Solomon was a
son of David and he built a Temple, but he is not the Son of
David and, as the chronicler sees it, a future Temple is yet to
be built (2 Chron. 36:23). David's hope that the promise
would be fulfilled soon, in his own day, was the same hope
that characterizes the godly of every generation. It was the
Son of David Himself who said, "What I say to you I say to
all, 'Be on the alert!' " (Mark 13:37).

a. The public announcement of Solomon's kingship
(28:1-10). The third announcement of the promise was given
as a public proclamation of Solomon's kingship before the
leaders of Israel. The account is without parallels in the other
historical books of the Bible. David announced that his plans
had been to build the Temple, but because he was a warrior
and not a man of peace, God had promised him a desendant
who would build God's Temple. Publicly, David announced
that God had chosen Solomon from among all his sons. As
long as Solomn remained obedient, God promised David that
his kingdom would stand firm (28:7). On the basis of that
promise, David admonished the leaders of Israel (28:8—the
imperatives are all plural, indicating that David was speaking
to the leaders) and Solomon (28:9) to keep God's commandments and obey His will.

Of special importance is the inclusion of the explanation
David gave for whole-hearted obedience: "for the LORD
searches all hearts, and understands every intent of the
thoughts" (28:9*b*). Because the chronicler is recording
David's establishment of the public and external forms for

worship, the Temple and the altar, the matter of internal, private sincerity is of utmost importance. It was, in fact, on this very point that Israel's covenant relationship with God foundered: "This people draw near with their words and honor me with their lips, but they remove their hearts far from Me" (Isa. 29:13). Public worship is of primary importance for God's people, but it can never take the place of a real, heartfelt relationship with God.

b. The Temple plan (28:11-19). David had received a plan for the Temple from the Lord (28:19), and now he passed the plan on to the builder, Solomon. The word for *plan* in Hebrew can mean either a "drawing" or a "set of instructions." As in the plan for the Tabernacle (Ex. 25ff), the meaning here is apparently a set of verbal instructions. Some idea of the contents of the Temple plan outlined by David can be seen in the description of the completed Temple (2 Chron. 3, 4). The plan itself is not included by the chronicler.

c. Work on the Temple Commissioned by David (28:20— 29:9). The chronicler takes great pains to make clear David's role in the building of the Temple. David's words to Solomon, admonishing and exhorting him to build the Temple, sound much like the words of Haggai, the prophet after the Exile, who "stirred up" the hearts of the people and the leaders to rebuild the Temple that had lain in ruins: "But now take courage, Zerubbabel," declares the LORD, "take courage also, Joshua son of Jehozadak, the high priest, and all you people of the land take courage," declares the LORD, "and work; for I am with you," says the LORD of hosts . . . "Do not fear!" (Hag. 2:4-5).

The chronicler was likely aware that the prophets in his own day, like Haggai, were in much the same circumstances as David had been. They saw the importance of the presence of God, and they saw the Temple as the embodiment of that promise. Their hearts burned with the zeal to build a house worthy of His presence, a Temple "not for man, but for the LORD God" (29:1).

In David's time a great freewill offering was made by the king and the people, and great quantities of gold and silver and valuables were donated for the building of the Temple (29:2-9). The beauty and splendor of the Temple was the mark of the splendor and majesty of God's glory, and a sign of the riches that come from Him (29:11-14). The king and the people rejoiced at the offering that had been given so willingly by God's people. But Haggai, as the chronicler, expected something even greater:

> For thus says the LORD of hosts, "Once more in a little while, I am going to shake the heavens and the earth, the sea also and the dry land. And I will shake all the nations; and they will come with the wealth of all nations; and I will fill this house with glory," says the LORD of hosts. "The silver is Mine, and the gold is Mine," declares the LORD of hosts. "The latter glory of this house will be greater than the former," says the LORD of hosts, "and in this place I shall give peace," declares the LORD of hosts. [Hag. 2:6-9]

At this point in the books of Chronicles, the writer has not yet reached the same level of expectation that characterizes Haggai's prophecy. He is content to let David and the people rejoice over the freewill offering of God's chosen. But as he later reveals, the magnitude of his hope for the future is equal to that of Haggai. The former Temple, glorious as it was, would not equal in splendor that later Temple to be built by the promised Son of David. As he describes the final ruin of that former Temple, whose valuables were stolen or destroyed (2 Chron. 36:18-21), his hope can be seen in his refusal to let the book end there. God's promises are sure and He is at work in the hearts of the nations. He has stirred up the spirit of Cyrus, king of Persia, so that he sent a proclamation throughout his kingdom: "The LORD, the God of heaven, has given to me all the kingdoms of the earth, and He has appointed me to build Him a house in Jerusalem, which is in Judah. Whoever there is among you of all His people, may the LORD his God be with him, and let him go up" (2 Chron. 36:23). This is nothing less than the same kind of hope as Haggai's seizing on the latest newspaper headline, Cyrus's decree. The chronicler sees in the edict of Cyrus the same range of expectation envisioned by Haggai. The former Temple was great, but whatever its splendor, a new Temple lies just ahead, incomparable in splendor to the former one and built by the "wealth of all the nations" (Hag. 2:7).

d. David's blessing (29:1-19). These are David's final words—his last address to his people and last official word to his son Solomon. It is no wonder that David chooses to review the central themes that have characterized his life and earned him the acclaim of being one "after his [God's] own heart" (1 Sam. 13:14, KJV).

The first of David's themes is the greatness of God (29:11-13): *everything* belongs to God. From acknowledging God's greatness David turns in amazement to what God's people have been able to donate willingly for the Temple. For David, God's power is seen in His enabling this people to build a Temple of such impressive value. David's words show that his thoughts have been dwelling on Israel's history, and that in its growth from a small family of shepherds to a kingdom of international importance, he has seen God's hand at work (29:14-16).

As his next words suggest (29:17), David seems to see, in the growth of the nation Israel, the course of his life's journey from shepherd to king. The nation's wealth did not depend on God's being impressed with the greatness of Israel, but in a God who looks not at the external appearance of things but who "looks at the heart" (1 Sam. 16:7). David's prayer

(29:18-19) is that the people and new king Solomon not lose sight of the centrality of a pure heart as they plan and build this magnificent Temple. The secret of David's leadership was not power and wealth, but trust in a God to whom belongs all power and wealth. As David had said elsewhere, the fear of the Lord is "more desirable than gold, yes, than much fine gold" (Ps. 19:10). For David, the people's willingness to donate all their wealth to build the Temple was a sure sign that their heart was pure. His prayer was that the Lord would preserve this intention of their heart. With that, David commits his people and their new king into the hand of his sovereign Lord.

e. The coronation of Solomon (29:20-25). A comparison of the accounts of Solomon's coronation here and in 1 Kings 1 shows clearly that the two books, while viewing the same event, have a different emphasis. The writer of 1 and 2 Kings, as the writer of 1 and 2 Samuel, is concerned with the conflict that lay behind the selection of David's successor. With both the rebellions of Absalom (2 Sam. 15-18) and Adonijah (1 Kings 1), the tension of striving after the throne is resolved by the wise counsel of the prophet Nathan (1 Kings 1:11-14). The selection of a successor to David was accomplished at great personal cost to David and his household. Ultimately, God's will prevailed and the man of peace, Solomon, ascended to the throne (29:22; 1 Kings 1:39). Assuming his readers are aware of the tragic details that preceded Solomon's coronation, the chronicler writes only of the final victory. That he assumes his readers know of the events of 1 Kings 1 is clearly seen in his notice that 1 Chronicles 29:22 is the "second" coronation of Solomon. The first coronation, before only David's entourage from Jerusalem, is recorded in 1 Kings 1. The second (29:22) is the coronation of Solomon before all the assembly of the leaders of Israel (28:1; 29:24).

f. The death of David (29:26-30). The account of David's reign ends with a notice of the years he served as king and a reference to other works that contain more information about the acts of King David. It is not clear if those works are the books of 1 and 2 Samuel and 1 and 2 Kings, or if the chronicler had other sources that are no longer available.

7

SOLOMON

III. Solomon and the Descendants of David
(2 Chronicles 1:1—36:23)

Solomon's major accomplishment was the building of the Temple in Jerusalem. The chronicler's interest in that aspect of Solomon's reign can be seen clearly by comparing the account of Solomon's reign in 2 Chronicles and 1 Kings 1:1—11:43. The Chronicles account is a shorter work overall and with few exceptions it includes only those events that serve to show Solomon's concern and care for the building of the Temple. In that respect, the chronicler's treatment of Solomon is similar to his treatment of David and his treatment of the Davidic dynasty in the remainder of the book. In recounting the deeds of the kings of Israel and Judah, the chronicler is concerned primarily with their care for the Temple of God.

Why does the king's concern for the Temple loom so large here? There are at least two answers to that question. First, by the chronicler's day the question of the Temple was perhaps the central issue of Israel's faith. The first Temple had been destroyed by the Babylonians. After the Babylonian captivity was over, the people returned to the land and the prospect of rebuilding the Temple in Jerusalem was in view. From the biblical literature of that period (the books of Haggai, Zechariah, and Ezra) it is apparent that not all Israelites were wholeheartedly in favor of the rebuilding of the Temple (Hag. 1:2-4). Certainly Israel's neighbors were set against it (Ezra 4:4-24). The godly leadership, however, clearly saw that if the people were to continue in their covenant relationship with God and continue to be in obedience to the ordinances given by Moses, they must have a place for worship and assembly. As the Lord had already said to Moses: "Let them construct a sanctuary for Me, that I may dwell among them" (Ex. 25:8).

The second reason for the writer's interest in the Davidic kings' concern for the Temple lies in the nature of the messianic hope in Israel. It is clear that the biblical prophets saw that Israel's only hope for the future lay in God's sending the promised King to rule the world in peace and righteousness (Isa. 9:6-7). The historical books (1 and 2 Sam. 1 and 2 Kings, and 1 and 2 Chron.) have provided the basis for that hope in the account of the Davidic covenant (2 Sam. 7; 1 Chron. 17). According to that covenant, the promised King (the Messiah) would be a descendant of David and would build a house (Temple) for God. The Messiah would not only be a political leader, but a religious leader as well. He would be king and priest, and although of the family of David and the tribe of Judah, He would not be of the priestly line of Aaron. Nevertheless, His concern for the proper worship and fellowship with God through the Temple would characterize Him as one who had priestly concerns.

King David epitomized that kind of king. It is clear that David was not that king, for David was a man of war and bloodshed, and the King to come will be a man of peace (1 Chron. 22:7-9). Nevertheless, David's kingdom characterized the kind of rule of the promised King. Henceforth, all kings in Jerusalem would find their measure in the degree to which they were like or unlike David. David's rule was characterized by a concern for the Temple worship. Indeed, the whole plan of the building and the order of the service was established by David's command. Thus, if a king was to measure up to David, he must have a zeal for the house of God (cf. John 2:17). It was part of the chronicler's primary concern to take a historical inventory of the descendants of David. He, in effect, asks: How did the promise to David fare? Did the promised seed come? Was God's promise fulfilled? His answer, although hesitant in the account of Solomon's reign, is a resounding no. There are good kings and there are bad kings in the inventory, but when the story has ended and the last king is in exile, the promised One has not yet come. The chronicler's concern, however, is not to lament the fall of the last king, but to point to the future to the One who is yet to come. Although a son of David, this king would have a dominion more like the great empires (Persia under Cyrus) of the chronicler's own day. His final note is the anticipation of the Davidic king who would rule from sea to sea (Ps. 72:8) and who, like cyrus, would announce that God has appointed him to build a Temple in Jerusalem (2 Chron. 36:23).

A. SOLOMON (1:1—9:31)

By any standards, Solomon was a great king. David had bequeathed to him a large and stable kingdom. The time of his reign came during a period of relative peace throughout the ancient Near East. The major empires of the past had exhausted themselves through internal political struggles, and the great empires, whose influence and military forces would soon sweep through the small kingdoms of Israel and Judah, had not yet begun their campaigns of expansion. Israel was left alone to carve out her boundaries among her many neighboring countries, and David's victories had settled, for the time, most of the issues at stake. It was left to Solomon alone to organize and administer the kingdom inherited from his father.

In this passage, the major interest is in how Solomon went about his task in one area: the building of the Temple. Since Solomon fared well at that task, this portrayal of him gives us reason to believe that Solomon might have fared just as well in other areas. He is seen at his best in the books of Chronicles. The writer of 1 Kings, however, shows that Solomon had major weaknesses in the character of his leadership. He was a man whose heart was not wholly committed to the Lord (1 Kings 11:4). A full picture of Solomon the man and Solomon the king would need to be drawn from both 2 Chronicles and 1 Kings, but that should not detour the reader of 2 Chronicles from appreciating the point of the chronicler. Whatever his weaknesses, Solomon had true greatness, and that greatness was seen in his devotion to the worship of God at the Temple. As a leader, he was concerned about his people's spiritual life. He devoted himself to providing for the presence of God among His people. In that respect Solomon was like the promised King.

1. *Solomon's preparation* (1:1-17). The first official act of Solomon was his journey to Gibeon with his entourage. His reason for going was that "God's tent of meeting" was there (1:3). Therefore, Solomon's first official act was in essence one of worship. The chronicler is careful to point out that worship at Gibeon was legitimate because all the accoutrements of worship prepared by Moses' instruction, except the Ark, were kept here.

The wisdom and wealth that characterized Solomon's kingship were a gift from God. It is important to see the nature of the wisdom that Solomon requested. He asked for wisdom and knowledge "that I may go out and come in before this people" (1:10). As his next statement makes clear (1:10b), Solomon was asking for understanding to rule (literally: "to judge") God's people. It is evident that both the chronicler and the writer of the parallel passage in 1 Kings had in view here the requirement of the king in Deuteronomy 17:18-20. The king was to know the law (*Torah*) of God and was to learn to fear God and observe all the will of God expressed in the law (*Torah*). In the words of Moses in Deuteronomy 4:5-8, the law is wisdom and understanding. Solomon knew the requirement of the king and asked God to make his heart conform to the Lord's will.

The significance of this account is to show that wealth and glory have value when they are reflections of a genuine heart attitude. The importance of a pure heart is not to be overshadowed by the splendor of the gold and silver of Solomon's Temple. The account of the building of the Temple poses the same question asked poetically by David in the Psalms: "O LORD, who may abide in Thy tent? Who may dwell on Thy holy hill?" (Ps. 15:1). The chronicler provides the same answer as David: "He who walks with integrity, and works righteousness, and speaks truth in his heart" (Ps. 15:2). Solomon was fit to be king.

As evidence of the Lord's answer to Solomon's request, the chronicler enumerates the wealth and glory of Solomon's kingdom (1:14-17).

2. *Preparations for building the Temple* (2:1-18). The natural resources and the technical skills of the Phoenicians were well known throughout the ancient world. Tyre was the place to go for building materials and skilled laborers. Although the chronicler, like the writer of 1 Kings, enumerates some details of the construction materials, his primary interest in the Temple preparations lies clearly in the written exchange between Solomon and Huram (or Hiram) of Tyre.

Solomon's letter to Huram provides a telling glance into Solomon's intention in building the Temple. If we had only the account in 1 Kings 3:17-19, we might think that Solomon built the Temple merely out of a sense of duty to complete the work of his father. The account, however, expands Solomon's purpose to include the desire to worship the God of the universe. Solomon saw the Temple, not as a place to contain the God of the universe, but a place where he and his people could celebrate God's presence. Solomon's letter also reveals his purpose for wanting the best craftsmen and the most precious materials: "the house which I am about to build will be great; for greater is our God than all the gods" (2:5).

Huram's reply to Solomon (2:11-16) is significant in light of the overall purpose of the books of Chronicles. One of the central themes is the place of the Gentile nations in the worship of God. Huram's reply to Solomon serves to show that even in Solomon's day there were Gentiles who recognized the Lord as the Creator and whose contribution to the Temple was welcomed by God's people. That is still a far cry, however, from Haggai's "wealth of all nations" (Hag. 2:7) or the vision of Zechariah:

> So many peoples and mighty nations will come to seek the LORD of hosts in Jerusalem and to entreat the favor of the LORD. Thus says the LORD of hosts, "In those days ten men from all the nations will grasp the garment of a Jew saying, "Let us go with you, for we have heard that God is with you.' " [Zech. 8:22-23]

3. *The Temple is built* (3:1—5:1).

The site of the Temple, Mount Moriah, is identified both with the threshing floor of Ornan, which David purchased (1 Chron. 21:18-30) and with the mountains where Abraham offered up his son Isaac (Gen. 22:2, 14). Since in Genesis 22:14 the theme is God's provision of a substitutionary sacrifice, the chronicler seems to be drawing on that by reminding his readers that Solomon's Temple site was on the same mountain. For sinful man to come into God's presence, a sacrifice was necessary. By grace, God provided the sacrifice.

No accurate picture of the Temple can be drawn from the books of Chronicles. This account of its structural details and furnishings is merely a rough sketch. The structure was long (about 90 feet), narrow (about 30 feet), and a little over 40 feet high—about the size and shape of a large suburban home.[1] The description gives the impression that the glory of the Temple lay not in its impressive size but in the quality and craftsmanship of its construction and furnishings.

Little can be said of the exact nature of many of the furnishings described in these chapters. Archaeological discoveries have brought to light temple utensils and furnishings from other cultures in the ancient Near East, but very little is available that can be positively identified with the Temple at Jerusalem.

The appearance and function of the two cherubim (3:10-17) is still a mystery, despite many different suggestions.

From the descriptions of the "cherubim" in Ezekiel 1:4-14 and 10:1-22, it appears they were angel-like creatures, sometimes with human features and sometimes with animal-like features. Certainly they had bodies, wings, arms, and legs and, at least in some cases, human faces (Ezek. 10:8, 14). We cannot automatically assume that Solomon's cherubim looked exactly like those in Ezekiel's vision. The term *cherubim* appears to have been a general term for any of a number of special beings. Complicating the entire picture is the fact that the term itself is taken over directly from the Hebrew word *cherub*, a word with no apparent derivation in the Hebrew language. English Bibles have simply taken over the use of the term from the early Latin and Greek transliterations.

---

1. John Gray, *First and Second Kings: A Commentary,* rev. ed. (Philadelphia: Westminister, 1971), p. 163).

In early Christian writings the cherubim were considered a part of the orders of angelic beings and in Christian art have generally been represented as rotund winged children draped in satin ribbons. It is safe to say that no historical importance can be attached to such a conceptualization of cherubim, even though the image of winged children still persists. Therefore only a general picture of Solomon's "cherubim" can be obtained with certainty: they were angel-like, winged creatures that guarded and symbolized God's holy presence. The purpose of the two pillars, "Jachin" and "Boaz" (3:15-17) also remains a mystery. From their description these two pillars do not appear to have been part of the structural support of the Temple. Instead, it seems they were free standing objects intended to mark the front entranceway to the Temple. In other words, like the Ark of the Covenant and the altar, the two pillars were a part of the Temple furnishings rather than a part of the building. As furnishings they played a role in visualizing the presence of God at the Temple.

The two pillars were beautifully decorated with capitals shaped like the petals of the lotus flower, over which was positioned a large globe decked with chains of golden ornaments. Because of the height (more than 30 feet) and position at the entrance to the Temple, these pillars would provide a vivid spectacle to all who came to worship in Jerusalem.

The most likely explanation for the names "Jakin" and "Boaz" rests in the Hebrew meaning. They probably were the beginning words of specific praises sung at the Temple. *Jakin* means "he will establish," and *Boaz* could mean "in his strength."

4. *The dedication of the Temple* (5:2—7:11). The chronicler gives the account of the Temple dedication in four parts: (1) the bringing of the Ark of the Covenant into the Temple (5:2-14); (2) Solomon's speech (6:1-11); (3) Solomon's prayer (6:12—7:3); and (4) the dedication ceremony (7:4-11).

a. The ceremony of the Ark (5:2-14). David had brought the Ark of the Covenant to Jerusalem (1 Chron. 16:1). At that time Jerusalem, called Zion, was only a small, well-fortified hill. Solomon built the Temple to the north of the city and extended the limits of the city to include the Temple. Consequently, it was necessary to move the Ark "up to" the Temple from its resting place in the city of David.

As was appropriate for the feast (Feast of Tabernacles) and for the occasion of the moving of the Ark, Solomon offered a great number of sacrifices, and all priests, irrespective of their duties according to the divisions (1 Chron. 24:1-31), had to be on hand to officiate.

After the Ark was positioned in the Temple, and a sound of praise was being raised in unison throughout the assembly, a cloud filled the house of God, marking the presence of the glory of the Lord (5:13-14). Henceforth, the Temple at Jerusalem was to be the place where God's glory dwelt. God's presence there became the basis of Solomon's dedicatory speech and prayer.

b. Solomon's speech (6:1-11). Once more the Davidic covenant promise was repeated (see chap. 4). This time Solomon expressly applied the promise to himself and his completion of the Temple: "Blessed be the LORD, the God of Israel, who spoke with His mouth to my father David and has fulfilled [His word] with His hands" (6:4; see also v. 10). Although Solomon was no doubt correct in his assessment of the Lord's fulfilling His promise to David that his son would build the Temple, he did not know that his own disobedience would lead to his downfall. He may have been the one in view in the promise, but he was not *the* One envisioned in the promise. The chronicler's purpose is not to show that the promise failed in the past, but to show why the promise still holds good for the future. Some explain that apparently duel application of the Davidic promise as a "double fulfillment"—a promise that had both an immediate and distant fulfillment. Another way to view the apparently double fulfillment is to note that the promise was conditional. When the promise was made, its fulfillment was conditioned by obedience. David said to Solomon: "As for you, my son Solomon, know the God of your father, and serve Him with a whole heart and a willing mind; for the LORD seaches all hearts, and understands every intent of the thoughts. If you seek Him, He will let you find Him; but if you forsake Him, He will reject you forever" (1 Chron. 28:9). When the conditions are not met, the promise remains to be fulfilled, but with a different person in view. The enumeration of the failures of the succeeding Davidic kings has its purpose in showing that the Person has not come who will fulfill the promise to David.

When Solomon said that the Lord "would dwell in the thick cloud," he was recalling a familiar image of God drawn from His appearance on Mount Sinai, "Moses approached the thick cloud where God was" (Ex. 20:21). The thick cloud represented the awesome presence of the living God in the midst of His people. Poetically, David had used that same image to picture the majestic power of God as a severe thunderstorm swooping down over his enemies to rescue him in answer to his prayer (2 Sam. 22:7-18). Another psalmist recalled the picture of God's dwelling in "thick clouds" as an image of His awesome acts of righteousness and justice (Ps. 97:2). The God in the "thick cloud" is like the storm that looms on the horizon with its awesome, impending power. Solomon's use of this image of God was no doubt prompted by the appearance of the cloud of glory that filled the Temple on the day of dedication. Behind this immediate cause, however, lay the whole tenor of Solomon's prayer to follow. In this prayer, Solomon presented the significance of God's coming to dwell at the Temple. He was not sitting idly by, but there to dwell *with* His people. He was there for fellowship, for help, and for judgment. As Moses told the people, "What great nation is there that has a god so near to it as is the LORD our God whenever we call on Him?" (Deut. 4:7).

c. Solomon's prayer (6:12-7:3). Solomon's prayer bears resemblance to two other great prayers in the Bible: Abraham's discourse with God (18:22-33) and Elijah's prayer at Mount Carmel (1 Kings 18:20-39).

Solomon's prayer resembles Abraham's discourse in its structure. Both prayers repetitiously drive home a single idea and seem to build toward a climax. The point of Solomon's prayer is clear: God is present among His people and hears their prayer when they, in obedience, call out to Him. This theme is stated at the beginning of the prayer: "O Lord, the God of Israel, there is none like You, O God, in the heavens and in the earth—You who keep the covenant and act in loyal love with Your servants who walk before You with all their heart" (2 Chron. 6:14). Solomon's enumeration of situations in which God's people may call out to Him culminates in the prayer of those who have been taken into exile (2 Chron. 6:36-39). The problem of the prayers of the exiles is important, as the conclusion of this book suggests. Although 2 Chronicles ends on the note of the nation in exile, the one ray of hope is the rebuilding of the Temple (2 Chron. 36:23).

The theological basis of Solomon's prayer is important to note. In Solomon's words, God's "name" dwelled in the house (Temple) he had built (2 Chron. 6:20). Solomon's idea of what that meant can be seen in his address to God in verse 18: "Will God indeed dwell with mankind on the earth? Behold, heaven and the highest heaven cannot contain Thee; how much less this house which I have built." God did not dwell in the Temple as men dwell in their houses. God was present in the Temple, but the whole universe cannot contain Him. Solomon was bringing together two important attributes of God. First, He is transcendent—the whole world does not limit Him. He is not limited to spatial boundaries. But God is also present. His presence can really be thought of as especially accessible at the Temple. That is what is meant by the phrase "put Thy name there" (6:20). To the biblical writers, the name of God, like His glory, was a way of speaking about God's attentive presence at the Temple. Solomon's choice of words shows that he has clearly thought the issue through: God, who dwells in heaven, hears the prayers given at the Temple, because there His name dwells (6:21). Even when His people pray toward the Temple in a far off land, God hears from heaven their prayers offered *at the Temple* (6:38-39). Such an attitude toward God's presence at the Temple was a hallmark of the King on whom the chronicler had set his hope (John 2:16).

In verse 17, Solomon says, "Let Thy word be confirmed which Thou hast spoken to Thy servant David." Solomon has already said that God's word to David has been fulfilled (6:10). Why should he now ask that His word be established? That comment by Solomon reveals that even he saw that the Lord's working in his own kingdom was not the end of the promise to David. Even Solomon acknowledged that more was to be expected from God's promise to David.

The conclusion to Solomon's prayer is the same as that of Elijah's prayer at Mount Carmel (1 Kings 18:38-39): "Fire came down from heaven and consumed the burnt offering and sacrifices; and the glory of the LORD filled the house" (7:1). The writer of 1 Kings does not include this dramatic conclusion to Solomon's prayer. He ends the prayer with a benediction (1 Kings 8:54-66).

d. The dedication ceremony (7:4-11). A seven-day feast for the dedication of the altar was coupled with the seven-day Feast of Tabernacles. The number of animals sacrificed during the dedication, though large, is not improbable. Even larger numbers of animal sacrifices are known from ancient times. As many as 256,000 lambs are said to have been sacrificed in Roman times.[2]

5. *Solomon's night vision* (7:12-22). Solomon received a confirmation of his prayer in a night vision (perhaps a dream). But he also received a stern warning of the importance of obedience to the will of God. Solomon's kingdom would be established if he was obedient to the will of God; if not, the nation would be exiled and the Temple destroyed.

The chronicler certainly knows that the Davidic kings were not obedient. His history has helped to make that fact indelible. But his purpose is not to rub salt in old wounds, rather his purpose is to show how to avoid the consequences of disobedience. When the nation suffers because of disobedience, the proper recourse of the people is repentance. God's people can always pray, repent, and seek forgiveness; He is always ready to hear and forgive (7:14-15).

6. *Solomon's kingdom is established* (8:1-18). In the preceding section, the Lord had appeared to Solomon and had reaffirmed the Davidic promise to him. When the chronicler recounted the initial promise to David (1 Chron. 17:1—21:30), he stressed several features of David's kingdom that demonstrated God's fulfillment of specific promises in the life of David. After the Davidic promise was reaffirmed to Solomon, the chronicler recounts several features of Solomon's realm that demonstrate the Lord's words "I will establish your royal throne" (7:18). Narratively, the chronicler has shown that God is faithful to His word.

7. *Solomon's wealth and wisdom are acclaimed* (9:1-28). Not

2. Edward L. Curtis and Albert A. Madsen, "A Critical and Exegetical Commentary on the Books of Chronicles," *International Critical Commentary* (1910; reprint ed., Greenwood, S.C.: Attic Press, 1977), p. 348.

only had the Lord given Solomon a great kingdom in fulfillment of the promise to David, but He also had given Solomon
much wealth and wisdom, as He had promised at Gibeon
(2 Chron. 1:12). Solomon asked first for wisdom, and God
also gave him wealth.

a. Solomon's wisdom and the Queen of Sheba (9:1-12).
Sheba, a land in southern Arabia, was essentially an empire
built on trading between the two continents of Africa and
Asia. The account in 2 Chronicles, practically verbatim that
of 1 Kings 10, serves to demonstrate the extent of Solomon's
reputation. Not only had the Queen of Sheba heard of
Solomon's great wisdom, but when she met him in person,
she discovered "the half of the greatness" of his wisdom had
not been told (9:6).

This picture of Solomon's fame and the distant nations
coming to hear him, bearing gifts, is reminiscent of the kind
of messianic hope characteristic of the chronicler's day (Haggai 2:7). Long before that time, however, in the eighth century B.C., the prophet Isaiah voiced much the same hope that
the Messiah's reign would show forth in such brilliance that
of His kingdom it will be said: "Nations will come to your
light, and kings to the brightness of your rising. . . . The
wealth of the nations will come to you. . . . All those from
Sheba will come; they will bring gold and frankincense, and
will bear good news of the praises of the LORD" (Isa. 60:3,
5-6). All nations will come to Jerusalem when the promised
Son of David comes. They will say, "Come, let us go up to
the mountain of the LORD, to the house of the God of Jacob;
that He may teach us concerning His ways, and that we may
walk in His paths" (Isa. 2:3).

The Queen of Sheba who came to Jerusalem with much
wealth and found that she had only imagined the half of the
king's wisdom gives a dramatic picture of the hope that the
chronicler, along with the prophets, had vested in the Davidic

kingship. What the prophets had voiced in their visions of the future, the chronicler narrated in his glimpses from the past. The rule of the biblical historians was "the future is like the past."

b. Solomon's wealth (9:13-28). The theme of Solomon's relationship to the other nations continues, showing how those nations contributed greatly to Solomon's wealth. Certainly Solomon's wealth was the result of good trade relations and wise use of resources, but it was something more. All of his wealth was the wealth of the nations, and they were bringing it to the son of David. The chronicler sums up Solomon's wealth: "So King Solomon became greater than all the kings of the earth in riches and wisdom. And all the kings of the earth were seeking the presence of Solomon, to hear his wisdom which God had put in his heart. And they brought every man his gift, articles of silver and gold, garments, weapons, spices, horses, mules, so much year by year" (2 Chron. 9:22-24).

Behind this portrayal of Solomon's wealth lay a clearly defined hope in what God will again do through the Davidic kingship. One like Solomon will come again, and the nations will bring their wealth to Him. "I will surely tell of the decree of the LORD: He said to Me, "Thou art My Son, today I have begotten Thee. Ask of Me, and I will surely give the nations as Thine inheritance, and the very ends of the earth as Thy possession" (Ps. 2:7-8).

It is well known that many of the Psalms make reference to circumstances in the lives of the Davidic kings of Israel's past. It is also recognized that their meaning does not end there. Even while speaking of actual Davidic kings, the psalmists often spoke of them in terms of the One who was to come. Events in their lives embodied the psalmists' vision of the future Messiah. Much of the treatment of David, Solomon, and later kings seems to be of that nature. In fact, in several important Hebrew manuscripts of the Old Testament the Chronicles are put before the Psalms. It is possible that the "messianic" treatment of David and Solomon in the books of Chronicles was intended to be taken as an introduction to the Davidic psalms.

8. *Solomon's death* (9:29-31). What is surprising about the portrayal of Solomon is that it concludes without any notice of the misfortune that befell him in his later years. The writer of 1 and 2 Kings put great emphasis on that point, making Solomon directly responsible for the division of his kingdom after his death:

> Now the Lord was angry with Solomon because his heart was turned away from the Lord, the God of Israel, who had appeared to him twice, and had commanded him concerning this thing, that he should not go after other gods; but he did not observe what the Lord had commanded. So the Lord said to Solomon, "Because you have done this, and you have not kept My covenant and My statutes, which I have commanded you, I will surely tear the kingdom from you, and will give it to your servant." [1 Kings 11:9-11]

Why does the chronicler omit those passages? Is he attempting to "whitewash" Solomon's kingdom? It is not likely that he would hope to cover up those unfortunate aspects of Solomon's reign. Throughout 1 and 2 Chronicles it is evident that the reader is assumed to be well aware of other biblical historical books and their treatment of the events. The chronicler even points the reader to further records of Solomon's reign in the conclusion to his account about Solomon (9:29). It is unlikely that he would hope to create a better picture of Solomon simply by omitting certain details from his account.

His reason for omitting those details seems to involve at least two factors. First, he assumed the details were known by the reader from 1 Kings and felt no need to repeat them since they were not important to his overall purpose. Second, his interest in Solomon was primarily "exemplary." Solomon was an example of *the* promised descendant of David who, in the chronicler's day, had not yet come. Insofar as the reign of Solomon represented the reign of the promised One, the chronicler's interest was served. He was content to let the other biblical writers give the more rounded picture. He was guided by his purpose, which was to build hope for the future rather than to lament the past.

One final note ought to be made: the validity of the message in large measure may actually depend on the reader's familiarity with the picture of Solomon recounted in 1 and 2 Kings. For the chronicler, none of the historical kings, including Solomon, fulfilled all the expectations of the promise to David. Some came close, like Solomon and Josiah, but none could be pointed to as *the* final fulfillment. That is the basis of the hope that underlies the chronicler's work—the true Messiah is yet to come. If, however, we had only 1 and 2 Chronicles, what basis would there be for saying Solomon was not the promised One? What basis would there be for saying he did not live up to the expectations of the promise as they are given in 2 Chronicles 7:17-19? There would be none, and the chronicler would be hard-pressed to explain why he was still looking for a fulfillment in the future if there is good reason to say the promise had already been fulfilled in the past. It seems unlikely that such a careful writer would have left such a problem unresolved. More likely, the whole question did not arise for the chronicler because he assumed his readers would know of Solomon's failure and of his disqualification as ultimate heir of the promise. That assumption of the chronicler's is what characterizes his method most distinctively.

8

DAVIDIC KINGS, PART 1
(REHOBOAM—JEHOSHAPHAT)

B. REHOBOAM (10:1—12:16)

Following his death Solomon's kingdom was divided. Ten tribes to the north rebelled against the Davidic dynasty in Jerusalem and established an independent state. For the most part the chronicler concentrates only on the Davidic kings in Jerusalem. He was seeking not a comprehensive understanding of the past but a theological perspective on the present and future.

1. *The rebellion of the northern tribes* (10:1—11:4). There are a number of interesting lessons to be drawn from this account (which is taken almost verbatim from 1 Kings 12). The first comes from the gist of the whole account, which is that Solomon's son Rehoboam did not act wisely and lost his kingdom. Taking counsel from the young men and rejecting the counsel of the elders is the ultimate in the lack of wisdom.

Another lesson has been inserted in the account: "So the king did not listen to the people, for it was a turn of events from God that the LORD might establish His word, which He

spoke through Ahijah the Shilonite to Jeroboam the son of
Nebat" (10:15). The course of events had been announced
beforehand by God, and Rehoboam's actions proved to be in
conformity to what the prophet had said. That insertion at
such a crucial point in the history of Israel played an important part in the overall message. Nothing can stand in the way
of God's purposes. What He has promised, He will bring to
pass. The reader is reminded that even a disastrous situation
such as the division of the kingdom and the loss of ten tribes
of Israel is not without its place in God's plan. By making
that point, the chronicler is giving his readers a basis for
understanding the Exile. If the loss of ten tribes was no threat
to the purpose of God, much less is the loss of the remaining
two. The Exile does not mean the end to God's plan. Ezekiel
made the same point in his vision of the dry bones:

> These bones are the whole house of Israel; behold, they
> say, "Our bones are dried up, and our hope has per-
> ished. We are completely cut off." Therefore prophesy,
> and say to them, "Thus says the Lord GOD, 'Behold, I
> will open your graves and cause you to come up out of
> your graves, My people; and I will bring you into the
> land of Israel. Then you will know that I am the LORD,
> when I have opened your graves and caused you to come
> up out of your graves, My people' " [Ezek. 37:11-13].

God will bring dry bones to life to establish His plan. The
word of the prophet remains firm. God will establish it. Included to reinforce that point is the account of the prophet
Shemaiah (11:2-4), who gave God's immediate revaluation of
the rebellion: "Return every man to his house, for this thing
is from Me."

It should be noted that because of the reference to the
prophet Ahijah the Shilonite, it was assumed that the readers
were aware of the account of the rebellion in 1 Kings
11:26-29. In that passage, the reason for the rebellion was
God's punishment of Solomon's disobedience.

2. *Rehoboam's kingdom* (11:5-23). The material covered in this section has no parallel in the other historical books. The section gives an important glimpse of the chronicler's evaluation both of the Northern Kingdom, Israel, and of the Southern Kingdom, Judah.

He clearly views the Northern Kingdom as having been led into apostasy by their new king, Jeroboam: "He set up priests of his own for the high places, for the satyrs, and for the calves which he made" (11:15). Thus, no one who still professed to seek the Lord could be a part of such worship. They must come to worship God at Jerusalem (11:16).

On the other hand, the chronicler not only views the Southern Kingdom, Judah, as the place of true worship, but he also sees it as now being made up of all those from all the tribes of Israel who worship the true God (11:16). It may be that the "remnant" of the true Israel, from all the tribes, has returned and that Judah is the true Israel. That would be implied in the words of the prophet Shemaiah: "Speak to Rehoboam the son of Solomon, king of Judah, and to *all Israel in* Judah and Benjamin" (2 Chron. 11:3, italics added); and it would be implied in the words of the chronicler: "And *all Israel* with him" (2 Chron. 12:1).

In the Southern Kingdom, little had been lost of the kingdom of David and Solomon. However, that would last only "three years" (11:17)—an ominous reminder that Rehoboam was not to be the promised One.

3. *Shishak's invasion* (12:1-12). The invasion of the Southern Kingdom by the Egyptian army under Shishak offered a lesson that could be well heeded: unfaithfulness brings punishment if you are God's people, "For whom the LORD loves He reproves" (Prov. 3:12*a*). The second part of the lesson is a source of great comfort: God looks upon a repentant heart with grace: "A broken and a contrite heart, O God, Thou wilt not despise" (Ps. 51:17*b*).

The military campaign of Shisak against Judah and Jerusalem was described by Shishak himself in a temple inscription in Karnak, Egypt. In the inscription, Shishak gave a list of cities conquered during the campaign, thus the event has been given independent confirmation by the Egyptian king's own records.

4. *The conclusion to Rehoboam's reign* (12:13-16). The summary of the reign of Rehoboam is to the pont: "He did evil because he did not set his heart to seek the LORD" (v. 14). That is, he did not properly worship the Lord by caring for the Temple and leading his people in God's law.

C. ABIJAH (13:1—14:1)

In contrast to the rather brief notice of the reign of Abijah in 1 Kings 15:1-8, the chronicler seems to have taken special interest in Abijah's short reign. The writer of 1 Kings grouped Abijah along with those kings who "walked in all the sins of his father which he had committed before him" (1 Kings 15:3). The chronicler, on the other hand, puts Abijah in a better light by virtue of his concern for the Temple, the priests, and the Levites. The chronicler undoubtedly concurred with the assessment of the writer of 1 Kings, but that did not prevent him from pointing to at least one redeeming act of Abijah.

Since Abijah's reign was characterized by constant warfare with the Northern Kingdom, the chronicler records the synchronic date of his reign with that of Jeroboam: in the eighteenth year of Jeroboam (915 B.C.), Abijah became king. Such synchronism of dates for the Northern and Southern Kingdoms is a regular feature of 1 and 2 Kings. It occurs only here in the books of Chronicles.

The account simply states that there was war between Judah and Israel, and that Abijah took the offensive, even though he was outnumbered two to one (13:3). Before the battle, Abijah made a speech that won him not only the battle, but also a place in history. In summary, Abijah said that Israel was guilty of apostasy because she had neglected the worship of God at the Jerusalem Temple and had set up a rival system of worship. The situation was tantamount, according to Abijah, to saying, "We [Judah] keep the charge of the LORD our God, but you [Israel] have forsaken Him" (13:11). Thus, Israel was fighting against the Lord by fighting against Judah and would lose (v. 12).

The account of the battle that ensued makes clear that Abijah's assessment of the situation was correct: "God routed Jeroboam and all Israel before Abijah and Judah. . . . Thus the sons of Israel were subdued at that time, and the sons of Judah conquered because they trusted in the LORD, the God of their fathers" (13:15, 18).

The issue at stake between the two rivals was not just a question of geography. It was not just a matter of the right Temple site. The question was, and is, a fundamental theological question: What is the basis of our standing before God? That is, is it something we must do or is it something God has done? God had chosen to dwell in the house made by Solomon in Jerusalem. It was God's choice, His will, that He dwell there and that Israel come there to offer sacrifices and worship. As Deuteronomy states over and over, God will be worshiped at the place where *He chooses* to dwell. God's presence could, and should, never be taken for granted. It is always an act of grace when He comes near to man in fellowship. The Temple site, chosen by God, was Mount Moriah—the place where *God provides* (Gen. 22:14). Jeroboam's disregard of God's choice of Jerusalem and his setting up of rival worship sites could only be interpreted as a denial of God's gracious gift and a substitution of human effort. God's presence was being beckoned by human enticement, as if God had need of man's worship and praise.

This chapter represents the primary statement regarding the

Northern Kingdom. The writer of 1 and 2 Kings has the Northern Kingdom in primary focus until its end in the exile of 722 B.C. (2 Kings 17). This chapter stands as the only assessment in 2 Chronicles of the "sin of the North." The chronicler then turns his attention away from the apostasy of the Northern Kingdom and focuses the remainder of his attention on the Davidic kings of the Southern Kingdom.

D. ASA (14:2—16:14)

The 1 Kings account of the reign of Asa has been considerably expanded in this section. Both authors agree at the start that Asa "did that which was right in the eyes of the Lord" (1 Chron. 14:2: 1 Kings 15:11). The writer of 1 and 2 Kings is content not to detract from that general assessment. However, the chronicler finds several features of Asa's reign that both support that general view and, to some extent, temper it with the picture of a reign characterized by spiritual defeat. The strength of Asa's reign lay in his concern for the renewal of the Temple and its worship and the courageous faith that Asa had in his Lord.

Asa had the good fortune to inherit a kingdom at peace, and he had the good sense to use the time to protect his kingdom from future war (14:5-8). Asa also had the insight to see that it was the Lord who had given his kingdom peace, and he took clear steps to maintain that relationship with God, for he removed the unlawful religious objects (14:3) and led the people in the lawful worship of God (v. 4). The "sacred pillars" and the "Asherim" were apparently forms of religious objects borrowed from the cultures of the ancient world. Little for certain is known about the exact nature and significance of those objects. The same can be said for the "horrid image" (15:16) set up by the queen mother.

1. *The invasion of Asa's kingdom* (14:9-15). No mention of this invasion is made in 1 Kings. The invader Zerah was an

Ethiopian, probably in the service of the Egyptians who held nominal control over the southern borders of Asa's kingdom.

The chronicler is interested in one aspect of the invasion—its demonstration of the power of God to deliver His people from the enemy. Although Asa was clearly outnumbered, he recognized in those unfortunate odds opportunity to trust in the power of God to deliver (14:11). The chronicler's summary statement tells the rest of the story: "So the Lord routed the Ethiopians before Asa and before Judah, and the Ethiopians fled" (14:12).

The central theme of that episode is stated in the final words of Asa's prayer: "O Lord, Thou art our God; let not man prevail against Thee" (14:11). Asa acknowledged as the basis of his trust and courage that man cannot hold back the plans and purposes of God.

2. *Asa's revival* (15:1-19). As with many religious revivals, the revival in Asa's day was started by the words of a preacher, the prophet Azariah. Azariah's message was straightforward: seek the Lord while He can be found (15:2). Azariah drew his lesson from the past and evidently had in mind the period of the Judges, although his description could fit many periods in Israel's history (15:3-7).

Asa's response to the message of Azariah was immediate. He, in effect, rededicated the Temple and celebrated the renewal of the covenant of the Feast of Weeks (Pentecost), which later Jewish tradition also used for commemorating the covenant.[1] Again, the emphasis was the direct connection between the king's spiritual leadership and his concern for the worship of God at the Temple. Here, Asa's actions were an intimation of the final work of the One who is to come (John 2:15-16).

---

1. Edward L. Curtis and Albert A. Madsen, "A Critical and Exegetical Commentary on the Books of Chronicles," *International Critical Commentary* (1910; reprint ed., Greenwood, S.C.: Attic Press, 1977), p. 385.

The chronicler's statement in 2 Chronicles 15:17 that the "high places" were not removed by Asa seems to state the opposite of 14:3: "He removed the foreign altars and high places." Several suggestions have been offered to lessen the apparent contradiction. A close reading of the text, however, shows that the problem is only an apparent one. The high places were not removed *from Israel* (15:17). In light of 14:3, it seems best to conclude that "Israel" here means the "northern kingdom" over which Asa had no control. That is clearly the meaning of the same phrase, "from Israel," in 15:9.

3. *The war with the Northern Kingdom* (16:1-10). Again the chronicler adds considerable detail to the account of the Kings (1 Kings 15:17-22), casting a shadow across Asa's victory over the Northern Kingdom.

The account of the war between Judah and Israel in 1 Kings is given without much editorializing on the part of the writer. The alliance that Asa made with the Aramean king, Ben-Hadad, might be viewed as a prudent venture that certainly proved successful. It might also be judged as a lack of trust on Asa's part; Asa chose to trust in foreign alliances rather than the Lord. In the context of 1 Kings, the second interpretation of Asa's alliance with Ben-Hadad is certainly more valid. The chronicler's inclusion of the prophecy of Hanani (16:7-9) shows that he, too, considers Asa's alliance with Ben-Hadad to have been an unfortunate mistake. As with the invasion by Zerah the Ethiopian, Asa should have trusted in the Lord, for the Lord would have delivered him (16:8). How easy it is, in Asa's shoes, to forget the help of God in the past and to falter in our trust in Him today. The prophet's words remain our only source of comfort as they should have been to Asa: "The eyes of the LORD move to and fro throughout the earth that He may strongly support those whose heart is completely His" (16:9). Curiously, Asa was angered at the prophet's suggestion that he had acted foolishly. His lack of trust in God resulted in his despotic oppression of his own kingdom (16:10).

4. *The conclusion of Asa's kingdom* (16:11-14). The conclusion of the acts of Asa calls to mind the final failure of the Davidic kings as a whole. Nowhere has that failure been stated more pungently than in the Lamentations of the prophet in exile: "Those who ate delicacies are desolate in the streets; those reared in purple embrace ash pits" (Lam. 4:5). Why did Asa's reign end in the shadow of God's judgment rather than in the light of God's help? The answer is given in the statement about Asa's diseased feet: "His disease was severe, yet even in his disease he did not seek the LORD, but the physicians" (16:12). Asa again failed to trust God.

Asa began his reign standing firmly in his trust in God. He ended his reign with diseased feet and a resolute refusal to seek the Lord. Certainly a part of the chronicler's intention in including this account of Asa's diseased feet was the picture it calls to mind of Asa's inability to stand firm.

E. JEHOSHAPHAT (17:1—20:37)

Jehoshaphat's name means "the Lord will rule [judge]." The account of the reign of Jehoshaphat seems to be governed by that same theme. All that he accomplished was based on the reality of a living God actively at work among His people, instructing them in the way they should go and defending them when they put their trust in Him.

Jehoshaphat's reign overlapped the reign of Ahab, the king of Israel. There were good relations between the two kingdoms as evidenced by the marriage alliance between Jehoshaphat's family and the family of Ahab (18:1). The marriage no doubt represented a political and economic alliance as well as a family alliance.

1. *Introductory summary of Jehoshaphat's reign* (17:1-6). The account of Jehoshaphat's reign begins with an assessment of the king that measures him by the deeds of David. According to accounts, Jehoshaphat did well.

2. *Jehoshaphat's administration of the kingdom* (17:7-19). In this passage we find a survey of the administrative accomplishments of Jehoshaphat. This survey is not included in the account of Jehoshaphat's reign in 1 Kings.

Jehoshaphat was concerned that his kingdom be properly instructed in the law of God. As his name implies, he desired that the will of the Lord might rule among his people, and so appointed officials and Levites to travel throughout Judah to teach the people the law (17:7-9). The people could not be expected to walk in God's way if they had never been instructed in God's will. Jehoshaphat was wise in seeing that instruction in the will of God must precede obedience. As he built walls to fortify his cities, so also he built spiritual walls to ensure obedience to God. Although those walls were not made of stone and mortar, they would still be standing long after the last bricks had crumbled in his fortified cities: "the word of our God stands forever" (Isa. 40:8). Jehoshaphat's concern is a clear example of the lesson of Solomon in Psalm 127:1: "unless the LORD builds the house, they labor in vain who build it."

The evidence of the Lord's approval of Jehoshaphat's reign is given by the description of the fear his enemies had for him. The enemies of Jehoshaphat did not make war on him because they feared the Lord. Their ancient enemies the Philistines even brought Judah "gifts and silver" (17:11). The chronicler has returned briefly to a common theme in his handling of the Davidic kings: when the promise to David is fulfilled, the nations will bring gifts to the promised One and they will live with Him in peace.

3. *Jehoshaphat and King Ahab* (18:1-34). This account of the alliance of Jehoshaphat and Ahab is almost verbatim from 1 Kings 22:1-53 and is centered more on Ahab than on Jehoshaphat. Jehoshaphat's actions here showed that his rule was guided by the will of God: "The Lord will rule."

The occasion of chapter 18 is a war between Ahab's Northern Kingdom and the Arameans over the disputed trans-Jordan lands around Ramoth-gilead. The unsuccessful attempt on Ahab's part to gain control of Ramoth-gilead was the third major confrontation between Ahab and his Aramean rivals. The battle ended with Israel's defeat and Ahab's death.

Jehoshaphat first made his mark on the situation when he insisted that Ahab inquire first for the word of the LORD before he went into battle (18:4). Jehoshaphat wanted to do only the will of God.

Not convinced that Ahab's 400 prophets had really spoken the will of God, Jehoshaphat insisted further that a "prophet of the LORD" be found to inquire of the Lord (18:6). Reluctantly, Ahab had the only prophet of the Lord available to him, Micaiah, brought before them and, as he had guessed, Ahab heard only an evil report from that prophet. Clearly the Lord was not with Ahab (18:16-22). Ahab's defeat that day in battle was confirmation that the words of Micaiah were true words of prophecy.

In taking over the description of the battle from the account in 1 Kings 22, the chronicler has added a small but very important comment. When Jehoshaphat was fleeing for his life in battle, having been mistaken for Ahab, he cried out and the Aramean captain saw that he was not Ahab and turned from pursuing him (1 Kings 22:32-33). To that brief account of Jehoshaphat's escape has been added the comment: "The LORD helped him, and God diverted them from him." It is clear from the 1 Kings passage that it was the Lord who saved Jehoshaphat, but the chronicler wants to ensure that the point is not lost.

This account of the alliance of Jehoshaphat and Ahab has been used for two quite distinct purposes in 1 Kings and 2 Chronicles. For the writer of 1 Kings, the account served to demonstrate the fulfillment of the prophecy of Elijah against Ahab because of his treatment of the Jezreelite Naboth (1 Kings 21:17-29). The writer makes that point explicitly at the conclusion of the account of Ahab's death (1 Kings 22:37-38).

For the chronicler, this account serves another purpose. It is used to show that God will deliver the king who calls out to Him and seeks to do His will. In the 2 Chronicles account, Jehoshaphat is seen doing both.

4. *Jehoshaphat's appointment of judges* (19:1-11). Jehoshaphat returned home safely after a close brush with death in the alliance with Ahab. When he returned home a prophet, Jehu, son of Hanani, was waiting with a word from the Lord: "Would you help the wicked and love those who hate the LORD and so bring wrath on yourself from the LORD?" (19:2). Jehu's words clearly referred to Jehoshaphat's alliance with Ahab and his close call with death. In light of Jehoshaphat's appointment of judges in this chapter, it seems likely that the chronicler also intended Jehu's words to apply to his present task. Jehu's prophecy is a fitting statement of the theme of chapter 19: Jehoshaphat's appointment of judges. The judges were to seek to administer the will of God among the people. Theirs was the awesome task of deciding between the guilty and the innocent. The judge was the representative of God and in his decisions he gave the will of God. It was of utmost importance, then, that the judge not align himself with the wicked by taking a bribe, but that he always carry out his work in "the fear of the LORD," that is, in obedience to the will of God alone (19:7).

Jehoshaphat's judges were a cross between a modern judge and an old-fashioned schoolteacher. Their task was not only to decide cases, but also to teach justice and oversee its application. Jehoshaphat's administrative system was modeled after that of Moses (Ex. 18:17-26). There were many local judges to decide minor cases, but he set up an appeal system as well, headed by the high priest in Jerusalem (19:5, 8, 11).

It is important to note that Jehoshaphat himself was actively involved in that system of justice and saw as his task the teaching and preaching of the word of the Lord (19:4).

5. *Jehoshaphat's war with the Moabites and Ammonites* (20:1-30). This event is recorded only here and truly typifies Jehoshaphat's reign and name: "The Lord will rule [judge]." The salvation of God is put in its clearest light in this narrative. As the prophet Jahaziel put it, "You need not fight in this battle; station yourselves, stand and see the salvation of the LORD on your behalf, O Judah and Jerusalem" (20:17).

The account of the prayer of Jehoshaphat is reminiscent of the dedication of the Temple by Solomon (2 Chron. 6:12-42). The nation was in danger of attack by its enemies, and the king rallied the people at the Temple to ask God's help. The basis of Jehoshaphat's prayer was God's promise to be present at the Temple and His promise to give the land to Abraham's descendants (20:5-9). His request was straightforward and could aptly fit the request of the godly throughout all ages: "O our God, wilt Thou not judge them? For we are powerless before this great multitude who are coming against us; nor do we know what to do, but our eyes are on Thee" (20:12). Jehoshaphat was not asking for vengeance; he was only calling on God for help.

The reply of the prophet Jahaziel reinforced Jehoshaphat's reliance on the Lord: "The battle is not yours but God's" (20:15). In those words we can hear not only the prophet speaking to Jehoshaphat and his people, but also the chronicler speaking to his own day: "Put your trust in the LORD your God, and you will be established. Put your trust in His prophets and succeed" (20:20). Surely God's people to-day need to hear that same word.

9

DAVIDIC KINGS, PART 2
(JEHORAM—JOSIAH)

F. JEHORAM (21:1-20)

The reign of Jehoram was a classic example of forsaking the Lord. He murdered his own brothers for no apparent reason. He followed the idolatrous practices of the kings of Israel to the north, to whose family he was related by marriage (21:6). His kingdom began to crumble before his own eyes as kingdoms on the east and west of him rebelled (21:8-10) and invaded his own kingdom (21:16-17). His life ended with a terrible illness, and when he died it was "with no one's regret" (21:20).

All of that was the result of Jehoram's forsaking the Lord and doing evil in God's sight.

Yet, there is another point to make in the account of Jehoram's reign. No matter how low the house of David may fall, God will not prove unfaithful to His promise: "Yet the LORD was not willing to destroy the house of David because of the covenant which he had made with David, and since He had promised to give a lamp to him and his sons forever" (21:7).

It is to be noted that Jehoram was not confronted by a prophet from his own kingdom, Judah. Unlike all the other

Davidic kings, Jehoram was opposed by Elijah, the great prophet whose call was to proclaim God's word against the apostate Northern Kingdom. What a comment on the wickedness of Jehoram that the prophet to the apostate Northern Kingdom should send a message against him as well (21:12-15).

G. AHAZIAH (22:1-12)

Ahaziah, like his father, Jehoram, and his mother, Athaliah, had close ties with the Northern Kingdom. His mother was the granddaughter of the Israelite king Omri and was the daughter of Ahab. The influence of his close relationship with the North and with his own mother ultimately meant destruction for Ahaziah (22:4).

This is a greatly abbreviated story of the end of the dynasty of Ahab that is recorded in 2 Kings 9 and 10. The chronicler has given only the facts relevant to Ahaziah's death. Because of his close association with Ahab's son Jehoram, Ahaziah was slain along with Jehoram by Jehu, God's anointed (22:7). That meant that Ahaziah's death was also "from God" (22:7).

Ahaziah was the only surviving son of Jehoram. When he died there was no one to succeed him from the sons of Jehoram, and so his mother, Athaliah, seized control of the throne. For six years, she reigned over the throne of the house of David; but in reality the true heir to the throne of David was hidden in the house of God (2 Chron. 10:1—12:16).

H. ATHALIAH (23:1-21)

Chapter 22 concludes with the notice that Athaliah ruled six years over the land. At the beginning of her reign she had killed all the heirs to the throne of David, with the exception of Ahaziah's young son Joash. Joash had been hidden in the Temple by his aunt Jehoshabeath, the wife of the high priest

Jehoiada. Chapter 23 takes up the events that marked the end of Athaliah's six-year reign and the enthronement of Joash. Because she was not a son of David, the chronicler is not interested in the events of the reign of Athaliah. It should not be forgotten that Athaliah was the daughter of Ahab, the wicked king of Israel (2 Chron. 21:6; 22:3).

The events of chapter 23 are crucial to the message of 1 and 2 Chronicles. For the most part, attention has been drawn to the role of the Davidic king in protecting and caring for the proper worship of God at the Temple. The fulfillment of the promise to David has been centered in the king's care and concern for the house of God. When the true, promised King comes, he will "build the house of the Lord."

The events of this chapter, however, have reversed the usual order of things. Now the king was not the protector of the Temple, he was the protected. The Temple was the vital link in the preservation of the Davidic dynasty. Without the house of God, there would be no Davidic dynasty, and hence, there would be no hope of the fulfillment of the promise to David. That reversal was not without its significance to the chronicler's own day. His day was much like the time of queen Athaliah's reign. A Davidic king was not on the throne. The hope of the fulfillment of God's promise to David rested on what was left of the house of David. Little could be done at the moment to restore the kingdom of David because Judah and Israel were no longer sovereign states. They were mere provinces of a massive empire, Persia. All that really remained of God's promise to David, for the moment, was the remnant of the house of David and the reestablished house of God. It is hard to say whether the Temple was complete in the chronicler's day or whether much still remained of its rebuilding. It is clear, however, that the focus of the hope of the fulfillment of God's promise to David was centered on the Temple. As long as the Temple remained, there was hope that Messiah would come to care for it. So, as in the time of Queen Athaliah, the Temple was the protector of the promise to David.

The reforms carried out by the priest Jehoiada after the death of Athaliah give some indication of the extent to which she had led the nation into false religion (23:16-17). The description of the nation's reaction to her death also suggests that Athaliah's reign represented a very low point in the history of the Southern Kingdom: "All the people of the land rejoiced and the city was quiet. For they had put Athaliah to death with the sword" (23:21).

I. JOASH (24:1-27)

The account of the reign of Joash, tragic as it is, provides a classic example of the lesson the chronicler has had in mind throughout these two books: God will fulfill His promise of peace by sending a son of David to reign successfully on the throne; his success will depend on his obedience to God's will; that obedience will be measured in terms of concern for the worship of God at the Temple. The priests and Levites were to play a central role in the promise because it was through their teaching the law to the king and the people that obedience was accomplished. Jehoiada, the godly priest, was able to lead the young king in God's will as long as he lived, but when Jehoiada died, the king and his kingdom fell into apostasy (24:2, 15-18). The lesson does not end here. When the people fell away from Him, God did not abandon them; He sent His prophets to warn them that they would be given over into the hands of their enemies as punishment (24:20-22). When the king and the people rejected the word of the prophet, God's warning of punishment came true (24:23-24).

Behind the tragedy of Joash's reign, however, there is the message of hope that pervades 1 and 2 Chronicles. If the people would listen to the prophets, if they would turn to God,

God would restore their blessing, and the latter glory would be greater then the former glory:

> And if Thy people Israel are defeated before an enemy, because they have sinned against Thee, and they return to Thee and confess Thy name, and pray and make supplication before Thee in this house, then hear Thou from heaven and forgive the sin of Thy people Israel, and bring them back to the land which Thou hast given to them and to their fathers. [2 Chron. 6:24-25]

The chronicler's work is like a great symphony in which recurring themes interweave and interplay; at one moment tragedy and despair dominate the scene, and at another moment, a brilliant hope lights the horizon. At no point in the book does either theme totally eclipse the other. Even in the darkest despair there is hope.

J. AMAZIAH (25:1-28)

At first glance the account of the reign of Amaziah appears sketchy and disjointed. A closer look, however, reveals that there are three carefully collected events from the reign of this king that deal with the issue of obedience to the will of God. Those events teach the now-familiar lesson of obedience: God helps His people when they obey, but when they disobey, God's people can expect punishment. The purpose of the punishment is to bring God's people back to Him and away from serving other gods (25:20).

The first event noted in Amaziah's reign is the justice carried out by the king against the slayers of his father (25:3-4). The chronicler draws an immediate point from Amaziah's actions to show that the king was, at the start of his reign, a good king—he obeyed the law of Moses (25:4; the law required that only the guilty individuals be held responsible for a murder, Deut. 24:16).

The second incident recounted from the reign of Amaziah is the battle with the Edomites, Judah's eastern neighbors

(25:5-13). In this account as well, Amaziah is shown to have been a faithful king. He obeyed the word of the prophet who warned him not to ally himself with the sinful Northern Kingdom. Although it meant less military strength, Amaziah went into battle without the help of the Northern Kingdom, and God gave him the victory.

In spite of those two accounts that show Amaziah to have been a king who honored God's word, whether in Scripture or in the words of the prophet, a third account is included to show that Amaziah's reign ended in failure because he did not continue to put his trust in God (25:14-24). In the midst of his victory over the Edomites, Amaziah met his downfall—he brought back the gods of the Edomites and set them up as his own gods (25:14).

The chronicler has wisely chosen the ironic words of the prophet to expose his utter dismay at the folly of idolatry: "Why have you sought the gods of the people who have not delivered their own people from your hand?" (25:15) The point of the prophet's words is simply that idolatry makes no sense. God had just delivered their enemy into their hand, and they responded by serving the gods of the enemy. The prophet's view of idolatry is much the same as that of Isaiah's who said of the idolator: "He feeds on ashes; a deceived heart has turned him aside. And he cannot deliver himself, nor say, 'Is there not a lie in my right hand?' " (Isa. 44:20). That God's people could forsake the living, personal God and follow an idol, was something the biblical writers could not fathom. It could only be explained as a result of the hardness of their heart. Amaziah's refusal to listen to the prophet's rebuke only emphasized the blindness of his idolatry (25:16).

Amaziah's blindness was a lesson in the dangers of idolatry, for Amaziah's defeat at the hands of the Northern Kingdom was "from God, . . . because they had sought the gods of Edom" (25:20).

This passage shows that the sin of idolatry was considered

extremely dangerous by the biblical writers. Idolatry struck at the very heart of the relationship between God and His people. The basis of the covenant was the personal fellowship between man and his Creator. The God of the covenant is a personal God. Therefore, the covenant meant a personal fellowship with God. Idolatry meant that an object, an idol, was put in the place of the personal God, and nothing was more of an afront to God than that. As He Himself instructed the people, "I, the LORD your God, am a jealous God" (Ex. 20:5).

K. UZZIAH (26:1-23)

Second Kings 15:1-7 gives only a bare sketch of the reign of Uzziah (Azariah), noting that "the LORD struck the king, so that he was a leper to the day of his death" (2 Kings 15:5). The chronicler has included much more material regarding Uzziah's leprosy to show that it was a result of the king's pride and presumption.

The first part of the account stresses that Uzziah's fame was well known and well deserved. He had built a great kingdom because he had continued to seek God. To seek God meant primarily to carry out the proper worship of God at the Temple. Behind the description of Uzziah's prosperous reign is the assessment that "as long as he sought the LORD, God prospered him" (26:5).

Uzziah's reign, however, took a decided turn for the worse in the account of the king's usurping the role of the priest (26:16-21). When Uzziah became strong, he became proud and no longer was careful to obey God's law (26:16). Only the priests were to officiate at the altar in the Temple (Num. 3:10, 38), but Uzziah dared to challenge God's will and, by force, set his mind to offer incense at the altar. The result of that act of rebellion was that the king was sticken with leprosy the remainder of his life.

The significance of Uzziah's leprosy is brought out clearly:

"He was cut off from the house of the LORD" (26:21). What a distance had been traversed from the promise of a coming son of David who would build a house for God (1 Chron. 17:12) to the Davidic king Uzziah who could not even enter the Lord's house because he was unclean. It is probably not too far off course to suggest that the emphasis on Uzziah's leprosy was sparked by the same realization that prompted Isaiah "in the year of King Uzziah's death" (Isa. 6:1) to say, "Woe is me, for I am ruined! Because I am a man of unclean lips, and I live among a people of unclean lips" (Isa. 6:5).

L. JOTHAM (27:1-9)

Jotham was a good king. He cared for the Temple (27:3), and his reign was recognized even by his neighbors (27:5). In summary, "Jotham became mighty because he ordered his ways before the LORD his God" (27:6). All of that should have added up to an important and influential reign. It is, however, surprising that the chronicler has devoted so little to the reign of this king. One clue to his treatment of Jotham may lie in the comment that "the people continued acting corruptly" during the reign of Jotham (27:2). Such a reign does not serve to build hope in the fulfillment of the Davidic promise. Jotham was a great king, but in his day there was no revival of the people. The kings that interest the chronicler are those who bring revival.

According to most interpreters, the comment that Jotham "did not enter the Temple of the LORD" (27:2) is to be understood in light of 2 Chronicles 26:16 where Uzziah acted presumptuously and "entered the temple of the LORD." Jotham, unlike his father, did not attempt to assume the role of priest by offering incense on the altar.

M. AHAZ (28:1-27)

At this point in the book, the narrative history is nearing

completion. There are still important moments ahead, but much history has been recounted and the major themes have been throughly developed. Much of the narrative has focused on the exemplary kings of the house of David. Weaker moments in the respective reigns of those kings have served primarily to point to the need for repentence and revival. The failures of the house of David have been kept to a minimum.

A new interest comes to the forefront with the account of the reign of Ahaz. On the not-too-distant horizon loomed the tragic final events of the kingdom of David—the Exile. The reign of the house of David was nearing its end and the promise had not been fulfilled. The chronicler prepared his reader well for that conclusion. At this stage in the book, the readers had come to expect that the fulfillment of the promise to David lay in a future Davidic King far removed from the present kings of Judah. The hope of the chronicler and his readers was not tied to the shifting moorings of the historical kingdom. His hope was in the One called the "Prince of Peace," whose kingdom will have no end (Isa. 9:6-7).

An important question still remains: Why must the kingdom come to an end? That is, why cannot the house of David continue until the One comes to whom it truly belongs? Why must the exile and destruction of Judah come?

The account of the reign of Ahaz provides the first evidence of the chronicler's response to that question. The account is by and large supplementary to the account of the reign of Ahaz in 2 Kings 19:1-37. Only three major events are selected: (1) Ahaz's idolatry (28:2-15); (2) Ahaz's appeal for help from the Assyrian king Tilgath-pilneser (28:16-21); and (3) Ahaz's sacrifice to the gods of Damascus (28:22-25). As the course of these events shows, Ahaz had a heart far removed from God. Although Ahaz fell short of God's will—something that all the kings did, including David—he did not turn to God in repentance when he fell under God's chastisement. On the contrary, God's chastisement served only to harden the king in his unfaithfulness: "Now in the time of his distress this same King Ahaz became yet more unfaithful to the LORD" (28:22).

Certainly there were other kings who did not heed the call of God and did not repent when they were punished. What is important to see at this stage in the narrative is that the chronicler has made a special point of bringing that feature of Ahaz's reign into the light. In doing so he is saying that the end of the house of David in the Exile was a result of the kind of hardness of heart exemplified in the reign of Ahaz. He is showing what David has said much earlier: "The sacrifices of God are a broken spirit; a broken and a contrite heart" (Ps. 51:17). Only when such a King comes will the walls of Jerusalem be rebuilt and will God again delight in burnt offerings (Ps. 51:18-19). Until then, the Davidic throne is better left idle than idolatrous.

It is certainly not by accident that the most vivid of all the Old Testament prophecies relating to the coming Davidic King (Messiah) were made during the reign of Ahaz (Isa. 7:1—12:6).

N. HEZEKIAH (29:1—32:33)

Although a large amount of material is devoted to the reign of Hezekiah, the main point of the narrative is simple: when the son of David cares for the house of God (Temple) and the worship of God there, God brings peace to his kingdom. The length of the treatment of Hezekiah's reign is because of the chronicler's concern for detail, which is his way of driving home his point. He gives a detailed account of the rededication of the Temple (29:1-36); the celebration of the Passover (30:1-27); and the reestablishment of the orders of service—priests and Levites (31:1-21). This revival of the worship of God is followed by one of the most stunning of God's victories in all of Scripture—the defeat of the Assyrian Sennacherib (32:1-33).

Hezekiah's reign, as it is depicted, appears to have sparked a new hope in the house of David. Hezekiah led the people in a genuine revival, and God heard their prayer and healed their land (30:20). The chronicler makes it clear, however, that he is not intending to rekindle a new hope in the present Davidic dynasty. Hezekiah grew proud, like many of the other kings, but he also repented and was forgiven. Nevertheless, his pride incurred God's wrath. Although his repentance averted God's wrath, such was the situation only during the days of Hezekiah's reign (32:26). The reign was not the time of promised peace, but rather, the calm before the storm.

1. *The Temple rededication* (29:1-36). According to 2 Chronicles 28:24, Ahaz had closed the doors of the Temple and had set up worship centers throughout Jerusalem and the other cities of Judah. Hezekiah's first important task was to open the Temple for worship and to reconsecrate it with a solemn assembly. Hezekiah's words spoke directly: "My sons, do not be negligent now, for the LORD has chosen you to stand before Him, to minister to Him, and to be His ministers and burn incense" (29:11).

2. *The Passover* (30:1-27). The revival that began in the heart of the king had spread to the leaders and was now proclaimed throughout the land. Hezekiah was especially interested in the survivors of the forced exile of the Northern Kingdom by the Assyrians. The chronicler does not recount the exile of the Northern Kingdom (2 Kings 17:6), but Hezekiah's proclamation to all Israel and Judah implies that the exile had taken place. For those remaining in the North and for those still in need of repentance in the South, the celebration of the Passover would mark the establishment of a renewed covenant and a return to the "god of Abraham, Isaac, and Israel" (30:6).

Hezekiah's proclamation to the North shows that repentance of the people would mean even a return from exile of many of those captives in Assyria (30:9). The basis of Hezekiah's call for repentance was the appeal to a God who is "gracious and compassionate, and will not turn His face away from you if you return to Him" (30:9).

Hezekiah's prayer for the people (30:18-20) allows a helpful glimpse into the heart of both this godly king and the chronicler who recorded the prayer. Both were sincerely concerned for the proper exercise of worship at the Temple. Carelessness in this regard would be the last thing either would tolerate. At the same time they both were concerned ultimately with the question of a right heart attitude. Mere ritualism is not the goal of Temple worship (30:19; cf. Ps. 15).

3. *The priests and the Levites* (31:1-21). Like David and Solomon before him, Hezekiah took a personal interest in the organization and welfare of the priests and Levites. The chronicler's particular interest seems to be to show that when the people tithe, there is abundance, "with plenty left over" (31:10).

4. *The invasion of Sennacherib* (32:1-33). The Assyrian Sennacherib was one of that country's most powerful kings. He led several military campaigns against the lands around Judah, and on more than one occasion his armies threatened the Davidic kingdom of Judah. Sennacherib recorded his version of the events in chapter 32 in his own royal archives. Although he boasted that he had Hezekiah trapped in Jerusalem "like a bird in a cage," it is clear that this boast was only a cover for a serious military defeat. According to the chronicler, that defeat was at the hand of the Lord's messenger in response to the prayer of His people (32:22).

Hezekiah's words of encouragement strengthened not only those in Jerusalem in his own day, but continue to give courage to failing hearts in every age: "Be strong and courageous, do not fear or be dismayed because of the king of Assyria, nor because of all the multitude which is with him; for the one with us is greater than the one with him. With him is only an arm of flesh, but with us is the LORD our God to help us and to fight our battles'' (2 Chron. 32:7-8).

O. MANASSEH (33:1-20)

The reign of Manasseh represents one of the most dramatic turnabouts in all of 1 and 2 Chronicles. Manasseh began as an extremely evil king and led the hearts of the people away from the Lord (33:2-9). Other biblical writers see Manasseh's reign as the point of no return leading to the exile:

> However, the LORD did not turn from the fierceness of His great wrath with which His anger burned against Judah, because of all the provocations with which Manasseh had provoked Him. [2 Kings 23:26]

> And I shall make them an object of horror among all the kingdoms of the earth because of Manasseh, the son of Hezekiah, king of Judah, for what he did in Jerusalem. [Jer. 15:4]

The chronicler, however, gives an account of Manasseh's repentance and reparations that resulted from a torturous exile to Babylon. What happened to Manasseh singly in his exile to Babylon was soon to happen to the nation as a whole. The chronicler seems to be drawing on the similarity of the two ''Babylonian exiles'' to show that even the most wicked offender can find grace when he humbles himself and calls out to God in prayer. Even Manasseh, the king most responsible for the exile, is an example of that theme: ''[If] My people who are called by My name humble themselves and pray, and seek My face and turn from their wicked ways, then I will hear from heaven, will forgive their sin, and will heal their land'' (2 Chron. 7:14).

Because the chronicler is more interested in the question of how to get his people out of the exile than how they got in, he dwells only on the results of Manasseh's repentance. Certainly Manasseh's early sins had devastating consequences for his people and his kingdom. In spite of Manasseh's repentance, the people still continued in his old ways (33:17), and his son Amon, the next king, multiplied the earlier sins of his father (33:23). The chronicler agrees wholeheartedly with the other biblical writers that Manasseh's reign and influence did mark the turning point to exile. However, he has left that point for others to make. For him, Manasseh's repentance is a dramatic lesson in God's grace.

P. AMON (33:21-25)

The reign of Amon was short, and both the writer of 2 Kings 21:19-26 and the chronicler devote little attention to it. The primary significance of Amon's reign lay in his failure to repent as his father Manasseh had. Amon's failure was a direct result of his father's earlier sins—the effects of Manasseh's sins continued to be felt among his people and in the life of his son Amon.

Q. JOSIAH (34:1—35:27)

The reign of Josiah was tragic. Josiah was one of the few godly kings of the line of David. He ushered in widespread reform throughout his kingdom, including the land to the north (34:6). At the peak of his reign, Josiah was slain in battle (35:22-24).

The account of the reign of Josiah emphasizes two important events: (1) the discovery and reading of the law of Moses (34:14-33); and (2) the celebration of the Passover (35:1-19).

1. *The law of Moses* (34:14-33). It is hard to imagine that God's people could have forgotten the law of Moses. Written copies of Scripture were not as common among the people as

they are today. The king was to have a copy himself (Deut. 17:18), and the Levites were to have ready access to their copies, but most Israelites probably learned the law of Moses from the teaching of their parents and the Levites (2 Chron. 17:9). The loss of the law then could occur in the span of one generation. All that was necessary was for one generation of leaders to neglect its responsibility to teach the younger generations. The loss of the law in Josiah's day was not a new problem. In fact, the problem appears to have been at the root of Israel's failure to keep her covenant obligations and to obey the will of God. Already in the earliest stages of her history as a nation, after the death of Joshua and his generation, "there arose another generation after them who did not know the LORD, nor yet the work which He had done for Israel" (Judg. 2:10). A new generation cannot live on a legacy. They must learn afresh who the Lord is and what He has done for them.

When the law of Moses was read, its words became the final sentence of God against His disobedient people: "My wrath will be poured out on this place, and it shall not be quenched" (34:25). The reference was to the coming Babylonian exile (36:17-21).

Josiah is seen as an exemplary Davidic king. He led the people in God's way and, "throughout his lifetime they did not turn from following the LORD God of their fathers" (34:33).

It should be noted again that the Temple was at the center of Josiah's revival. It was as the people were repairing the Temple that they discovered the law. As the Temple once protected the house of David (2 Chron. 22:10-12), so now it protected the law of Moses. The Temple had preserved from destruction the two foundational pillars of Israel's faith, the law and the king. It also served as the rallying point of Israel's faith in the coming Messiah. The God whose name dwells at the Temple is a living God and has promised to send an eternal King to rule His kingdom in peace and righteousness. Even as the people came to worship at the Temple in the chronicler's day, the hope of the promised Messiah dominated their praise and singing:

> The LORD has sworn to David, a truth from which He will not turn back; "Of the fruit of your body I will set upon your throne. If your sons will keep My covenant, and My testimony which I will teach them, their sons also shall sit upon your throne forever." For the Lord has chosen Zion; He has desired it for His habitation. This is My resting place forever; here I will dwell, for I have desired it. I will abundantly bless her provision; I will satisfy her needy with bread. Her priests also I will clothe with salvation; and her godly ones will sing aloud for joy. There I will cause the horn of David to spring forth; I have prepared a lamp for Mine anointed. His enemies I will clothe with shame; but upon himself his crown shall shine. [Ps. 132:11-18]

2. *The Passover* (35:1-19). Again the intensity of the chronicler's interest in Josiah's care for the worship of God at the Temple can be measured in his attention to detail. Josiah's reign pictures vividly the reign of the coming King. When He comes, He will be like Josiah. He will lead His people in the worship of God at the Temple.

3. *The death of Josiah* (35:20-27). The chronicler is not concerned with the details of the battle that resulted in Josiah's death. The battle at Carchemish involved two major empires of the ancient Near East, Babylon and Egypt. Josiah met his end while attempting to oppose the Egyptian forces en route to the battle. Because Josiah did not listen to Neco's message, he was killed in the battle that ensued (35:23-24). Josiah, a great king whose reign was characterized by obedience and godliness, in the end did not heed God's warning and fell in

battle. At this last moment in his book, the chronicler has reminded his readers that the promised seed of David has not yet come. Even Josiah failed at a crucial moment to obey the will of God. The words of David regarding the promise of an eternal kingdom lie behind Josiah's tragic end: "If you seek Him, He will let you find Him; but if you forsake Him, He will reject you forever" (1 Chron. 28:9).

CONCLUSION

R. THE CONCLUSION (36:1-23)

Having completed the account of Josiah, the last exemplary Davidic king, and having already had occasion to draw the important lesson of disobedience from the ungodly Davidic kings, the chronicler brings his work to a rapid conclusion. Second Chronicles ends with a cursory review of the last of the kings who reigned over the kingdom of their father David (36:1-13); a short sermon on the cause of the exile (36:14-21); and the edict of Cyrus, marking the start of the Temple rebuilding (36:22-23).

1. *The last kings* (36:1-13). The chronicler's emphasis in recounting the days of the last Davidic kings is to show that their dominion was finished and that the real power now rested in the hands of foreign empires—Egypt and Babylon. What a great distance from the expectation that the Son of David would rule from sea to sea with the nations as His inheritance (Ps. 2). The point is that the historical kingdom of David was not the reign envisioned in the promise to David. That kingdom ended in failure. To explain that further, a concluding sermon is added to this account of the last kings—kings whose reigns typified much of the house of David before them.

114

2. *The chronicler's sermon* (36:14-21). The theme of the chronicler's concluding remarks is expressed awesomely in 36:16: "They continually mocked the messengers of God, despised His words and scoffed at His prophets, until the wrath of the LORD arose against His people, until there was no remedy." God gave His people over into the hands of their enemies, and those enemies burned the house of God (v. 19) and carried His people into captivity in Babylon (v. 20). All that is the opposite of what the chronicler hopes for. The past lies in the ruins he is now describing, but the future lies in the promise of God: "[If] My people who are called by My name humble themselves and pray, and seek My face and return from their wicked ways, then I will hear from heaven, and will forgive their sin, and will heal their land" (2 Chron. 7:14).

When the Temple is again rebuilt and the people pray, even though they are in exile (2 Chron. 6:36-39), God will hear their prayer and restore their peace. All is made to rest on the rebuilding of the Temple. Had the chronicler ended his work here, there would have been little hope for the future because the Temple lay smoldering in ruins. The chronicler, therefore, concludes on an entirely different note—not one of despair, but one of hope. It is a hope built on the latest news flash from the "world press international"—the edict of Cyrus ordering the rebuilding of the Temple in Jerusalem.

3. *The edict of Cyrus* (36:22-23). The last two verses of 2 Chronicles ultimately determine the mood of both books. They are not about the failure of man, but about the power and promises of God. Out of the ruins of human effort, the chronicler shows that God's purposes can never fail and that all He purposes to do will be accomplished. Isaiah states it well: "the zeal of the LORD of hosts will accomplish this" (Isa. 9:7).

The Exile and destruction of the Temple may have seemed to put an end to the promise that God would rule His people through the house of David, but the chronicler's purpose has been to show that God is still at work and the hearts of the mightiest rulers are in His hand. If need be, God will stir up the spirit of Cyrus, the king of Persia, to accomplish His purpose, and the edict of Cyrus, published in the chronicler's day, seems to him to be just such an occasion (see Isa. 44:28). God is at work in history and in the course of events that are shaping history. What some may have read as an interesting and much welcomed headline, the chronicler sees as proof that God's "compassions never fail. They are new every morning; great is Thy faithfulness" (Lam. 3:22-23).